SIZE
DOES
MATTER

R.A. VERNON

Victory Media & Publishing Company
16781 Chagrin Boulevard #132
Cleveland, Ohio 44120
www.victorymp.com

Printed in the United States of America

/ ACKNOWLEDGMENTS /

First, I thank God for the precious privilege of being used in His Kingdom. He has blessed me with unusual favor both in my family and ministry and for that I am humbled and grateful.

To my pastor and spiritual covering, Bishop Joey Johnson, your love and guidance has made me both a better pastor and leader for my family.

I'd also like to thank my spiritual daughter, Jennifer Wingfield. Who would have thought 25 years ago when you were sitting in my Wednesday night Bible study at 5 years old in the basement of a little Baptist church, that you'd be my Executive Assistant in a megachurch editing my book? Wow!

I would also like to thank Larry and Andritta Craig. You guys have been serving my family and me for over a decade. You loved us before anybody knew our name and for that I am eternally grateful.

I love and thank the members of "THE WORD" CHURCH. Without your giving and support I'm not sure the life my family and I live would be a reality. I am almost ashamed to admit that I don't even know the total cost of my seminary education because I have never seen a bill. I'm exceedingly blessed to have a church that would invest in me. "THE WORD" CHURCH is the last place I plan to pastor in my life.

Finally, I would like to thank my wife and my children for their sacrifice over the last five years. Thanks, Ralph and Ray, for letting Daddy study when I should have been outside playing with you guys. Thanks, Victory, for being my wife and my strongest supporter. Whenever the pull of megachurch ministry and seminary overwhelmed me, you wouldn't let me skip a class or miss a paper. Thank you for your strength and support. As Forrest Gump told Jenny, "You're my girl!"

/ FOREWORD /

In my leadership consultations with literally thousands of pastors, including a few hundred megachurch pastors, I've discovered that while most place the emphasis on the word 'church' in the descriptor 'megachurch', the emphasis should be on 'mega'.

In a megachurch, the pastor experiences mega joys and mega pains; mega possibilities and mega pitfalls; mega opportunities and mega disappointments—it becomes all things mega. I've also observed that mega is a great exaggerator. It blows everything, good and bad, out of proportion and by the time the "news" spreads, it has spread by mega factors.

Managing and leading the mega of a megachurch is the central message of Dr. R. A. Vernon's book that you now hold in your hands. *Size Does Matter* is a transparent journey of one pastor's life. As you extract what's applicable to you, it will help you both theoretically and pragmatically.

In this book, you will find help in areas of frustrations as the number of your peers might be diminishing and you find fewer people you can turn to for credible and trusted counsel. Dr. Vernon discusses the theology of people (who you're called to), theology of place (where you're called to) and theology of purpose (what you're called to).

The never ending challenges of megachurches as it relates to the assimilation of new people, managing the ever-increasing need for more facilities, and providing pastoral care is rarely understood by those envying megachurch pastors.

You will also be challenged by the pragmatic approach Size Does Matter takes in describing marketing, finances, facilities, multiple services, multiple sites and other practical issues discussed in a simple, how-to format.

Increasing numbers of attendees increases resources, thus the capacity to deliver on the needs represented in the community. All this translates to higher accountability and greater focus on issues of stewardship that megachurches must embrace.

When the church of Jesus Christ had its grand opening and went public on the day of Pentecost in Acts 2, it began as a megachurch! The first new members class had 3,000 (Acts 2:41), the next new members class had 5,000 (Acts 4:4), and soon they stopped counting and simply called them the multitude (Acts 4:32).

Megachurches are as old as the church itself because God understands that Size Does Matter.

Dr. Samuel R. Chand

/ PREFACE /

Size Does Matter is a potent response to the controversy and myths surrounding the megachurch, its purpose, and its plight. For years, especially in the African-American church, the perception has been that the selfish ambition of the megachurch is to be a money-driven, personality-centered institution that does little to meaningfully help those in need. Using "THE WORD" CHURCH as my primary example, I puncture these myths as universal truths and postulate a polemic on exactly why pastors should want to reach mega propor-tions—for the sake of supporting the least, the lost, and the left out. The more human and monetary resources you have, the more you can do to spiritually, educationally, socially, and economically affect positive change in your community.

In addition to saving the lost, the single, most important reason megachurches should exist is to fulfill the call of Matthew 25:35-36, "'For I was hungry, and you gave Me something to eat; I was thirsty, and you gave Me something to drink; I was a stranger, and you invited Me in; naked, and you clothed Me; I was sick, and you visited Me; I was in prison, and you came to Me.'"

Furthermore, in this book I present step-by-step instructions specifically for pastors and church leaders desiring to grow their ministry, but marginally, for entrepreneurs, small business owners, and career professionals looking for solid methods to help them enhance their level of service and increase their company's consumer appeal. The advice and experiences I share are insightful and honest, as I chronicle my successes and failures from both a ministry and personal perspective.

It is no secret that megachurches have increasingly gained mainstream popularity among Generation X and many other demographics of churchgoers. Parishioners are pleased with the plentiful parking and satisfied with the series being preached by pastors with whom they can identify. They are impressed with the programs, resources, ministries and services offered. They are glad to be a part of a church that shows progress, promise, and a growing population, and are grateful to have their children taught and engaged on age-appropriate levels.

However, the increasing popularity of megachurches when viewed through the lenses of many pastors with smaller churches tells a slightly different story. Megachurches seem attractive based on common misconceptions related to the amount of offerings perceived to be taken in, the flocks of people frequenting every weekend, the national and international ministry television programs, the celebrity of megachurch pastors, and just the hype overall. Oftentimes, those pastors who desire to reach megachurch magnitude really have no idea what challenges accompany the task. From conversations I have had with hundreds of pastors across the nation, I know that many of these pastors are disillusioned and have a diluted purpose for wanting to be mega.

What I advance in *Size Does Matter* is that the purpose of having large numbers is not simply for numbers' sake, but rather for the sake of helping the marginalized and indigent. Church leaders' desire for growth should directly correlate to their desire to win souls for Christ as well as their desire to holistically impact the community. The more members you gain (once they have been properly trained in giving), the more money your church will have. An increase in funds will enable more outreach and evangelism, ultimately leading to the winning of souls for the kingdom.

The secondary reason I wrote this book was to help eradicate many of the misconceptions associated with being mega, and in tandem with my first and second objectives, I want to make sure I emphasize the importance of developing and growing your church. While the reality is that every church will not be a megachurch, that truth should not preclude any pastor from pursuing ways of increasing their attendance and finances. In this book, I encourage pastors and church leaders to do whatever they can to grow their church, and as a part of my effort, I offer practical, applicable advice to help them achieve that goal.

At present, I am a pastor of a megachurch, but I was raised in a much smaller, traditional church, and I transitioned from the latter to the former as if it were a Christian continuum, seeing how "THE WORD" CHURCH grew by the thousands every year since our inception in 2000. As a result, I know experientially what works and what does not, and what we as spiritual leaders have to do to remain relevant and keep winning souls for Christ.

However, I also know the importance of incorporating the views, research, and theories of other church leaders and biblical scholars in order to properly situate my position in the current discourse surrounding the megachurch phenomenon, and to avoid positing a biased view based solely on my personal experience. This understanding was the intellectual premise for writing this book. The spiritual premise was birthed out of my vocational responsibility to share as much as I can to help further spread the Gospel of Jesus Christ, and pastors, if you find even a fraction of what I offer in this book helpful to you, then I am comfortable that I am fulfilling my obligations.

Size Does Matter is an expanded version of my doctoral dissertation, based on the data I collected regarding church growth and the evaluations of my project that were completed by independent sources. The step-by-step format, coupled with quotes from respected church leaders and my own shared experiences, balances proof—substantiated evidence lending credence to my beliefs—with purpose—why a church leader should be interested in seeing the attendance of their church increase.

From my dissertation research, I was able to conflate data on different aspects of ministry, and paint a picture of inhibitors and exponents of church growth. I elaborate extensively on some of the more pragmatic but sometimes overlooked areas of ministry such as customer service, organization, and infrastructure. It is important to note that the worship experience cannot be separated from these critical subjects. I have found that people respond better when they feel loved, valued, and appreciated. People also respect order. There is a measurable connection to the unassailable advantage of organized leadership and sound ministry structure with church growth or lack thereof, but I'll speak more on that later.

The philosophies that I share in this book are tried and true. I have experienced, through a series of decisions (both wise and unwise), what leads to church growth and what hinders it. Every single chapter covers a different area of ministry. I present the moral and methodical maxims that have worked for me in a way that can be easily grasped and put into practice regardless of what level of ministry you are on. I also strongly suggest exploring some of the more experience-based texts I reference throughout (The Total Money Makeover, Cracking Your Church's Culture Code, The Creative Leader, etc.) for deeper study, and increased understanding on what it takes to develop a megachurch, and churches in general.

Whether you are just beginning to embark on the journey of the pastorate, you've been pastoring 20 years, or even if you're a young executive or aspiring business owner in need of some practical principles to help strengthen and cultivate your business, it is my belief and hope that *Size Does Matter* will help you lead and grow your organization with passion, promise, and purpose.

SIZE DOES MATTER

CHAPTER ONE

/ SO YOU WANT TO BE MEGA /

Each year, hundreds of pastors from across the nation and a few from other countries come to "THE WORD" CHURCH in Cleveland, Ohio for our Gathering of The Shepherds Pastors and Leaders Training. These wonderful men and women of God invest in their desire to learn from our ministry by paying registration costs along with travel and accommodations for not only themselves and their spouses, but also for staff and key leaders in their ministries. They come for an amalgam of reasons, chief of which is to acquire strategies that will help their churches grow numerically and financially.

Many pastors watch me and other megachurch leaders on television and admire from afar the large crowds, facilities, and popularity of the megachurch in general. I often tell my congregation that I love leading a megachurch and wouldn't trade it for the world. At the same time, I would not recommend this job to anyone who is not graced for it. There are many myths, both positive and negative, regarding megachurches and the unique men and women who lead them. In their book *Beyond Megachurch Myths*, Scott Thumma and Dave Travis do a thorough job of tackling many of the untruths and ambiguities regarding these large places of worship and what people think they know about them. That said, I feel no need to redo that work. Instead, I would rather give pastors who desire to lead a large or mega congregation some step-by-step principles that I believe helped our church grow.

The average church in America has a hundred or less people in it. Thumma and Travis define megachurch as "simply a Protestant church that averages at least 2,000 total attendees in their weekend services."[1] According to the data from one study, shown in the chart below from The Hartford Institute for Religious Research, there is only a myopic amount of megachurches when compared with others.

Approximate Distribution of U.S. Protestant and Other Christian Churches by Size (Excluding Catholic/Orthodox)

ATTENDANCE	# OF CHURCHES	WEEKLY WORSHIPERS	PERCENT
7-99	177,000	9 million	59%
100-499	105,000	25 million	35%
500-999	12,000	9 million	4%
1,000-1,999	6,000	8 million	2%
2,000-9,999	1,170	4 million	0.4%
10,000+	40	0.7 million	0.01%
TOTALS	Approx. 300,000	Approx. 56 million	100%

---

1. Thumma, Scott and Dave Travis, Beyond Megachurch Myths, (What We Can Learn from America's Largest Churches, (San Francisco: Jossey-Bass, 2007), xvi

Though megachurches are increasing at a rate of about 50 a year, that's still a relatively small amount when compared to the national averages.[2] The reality is, most pastors reading this or any other book on church growth will never be mega. Nevertheless, it is my contention that many churches could be larger than they presently are if they are willing to make some adjustments to their style, ministry methods, and development strategies. If you are ready to work at growing your church and possibly becoming mega, there are some things you definitely need to know.

WELCOME TO THE 21ST CENTURY

When I was growing up in the '70s and '80s, everybody went to the "family" church. Whether the pastor could preach or not was beside the point; he was the pastor that had done the hatching, matching, and dispatching for the family. Hatching—he dedicated all the babies that were born in the family; matching—he did the ceremonies of whoever got married in the family; dispatching—he did the eulogies of everyone who died in the family. Because of the pastor's involvement in the personal lives of almost the entire family, everyone felt a certain allegiance to both him and the family church. No matter how boring or irrelevant the sermon was, and despite the fact the worship was tailored to the taste of the seniors of the church who had grown up in church and liked traditional hymns and anthems, we came anyway because it was all we knew.

In the mid-90s, when megachurches started appearing, the Generation X crowd in these traditional churches broke precedence by leaving the family church in search of something more conducive to their needs. For the first time in the Black Church's recent history, children were worshiping in a different place than their parents.

---

2. Thumma, Scott and Dave Travis, Beyond Megachurch Myths, (What We Can Learn from America's Largest Churches, (San Francisco: Jossey-Bass, 2007), 7.

Today people shop for churches. They want to know what you have to offer. How is the parking? What programs do you have for children? Do you have a workout facility and gym? Because of their size, large churches and megachurches alike are able to meet many of the needs that smaller churches cannot.

GROWING PAINS

Though I love leading a megachurch, it is critical that pastors experiencing exponential growth and those with aspirations of becoming mega understand some of the challenges that accompany this task. No matter how easy it looks on TV, leading churches of this size is an extremely arduous and stressful job. Dr. Samuel Chand, a good friend and expert in the area of church leadership, helps hundreds of pastors across the nation including megachurch leaders. In his book *Cracking Your Church's Culture Code*, referencing senior pastors in general, he says this:

> *I believe that the role of senior pastor is the most glorious and at the same time the most difficult in the world. These leaders have the incredible privilege of representing the King of Kings, imparting grace and life to people and creating environments in which God's spirit changes the eternal destiny—and the present relationships and direction—of men and women, boys and girls in the community. There is no higher calling. Yet senior pastors shoulder enormous burdens. They have to be "on" every time they speak, whether it's to the entire congregation or to an individual. They feel the pressure of finances, deadlines, new visions and missed opportunities, the mistakes and sins of their staff, and their own flaws. But even as they face those troubles, they are expected to be the source of hope, peace, and wisdom for every person in their world.*[3]

---

3. Chand, Samuel, Cracking Your Church's Culture Code, (San Francisco: Jossey-Bass, 2011), 6.

As true as Chand's assessment is for all senior pastors, it is immensely magnified for those of us who lead megachurches. The stress of leading thousands of people and dealing with a multimillion-dollar budget can be so overwhelming that it causes both mental and physical sickness. As I will discuss in a later chapter, one of the ongoing issues of leading a megachurch is that you are constantly dealing with the good problem of growth. Where will I park parishioners and where will they sit? Should I start another service? Is God saying to open a second location? OK, now should I open a third? Heck, we are still growing, should I open a fourth one? I know these sound like problems a pastor frustrated by small numbers would love to have and by no means am I suggesting I would like to switch, but as my grandmother used to say, "Everything that glitters ain't gold!"

As you grow, you will find that you need more people to assist you. The problem is that fast growth triggers feelings of apprehension and prompts anxiety-driven decision-making. Because things are happening so quickly, you feel pressure to employ people to fill positions that may require more training, education, or experience than they have. I'll speak more on this when I deal with my chapter on staffing, but impetuously hiring or selecting individuals to help you will inevitably lead to regret on some level. In my personal experience, making hasty hiring decisions has led to betrayal, moral failures, and a laundry list of other setbacks that accompany promoting people prematurely.

LONELINESS

Have you ever heard the adage, "It's lonely at the top?" There are times when I feel there is no truer saying in the world, especially when I scroll through hundreds of numbers in my cell phone after a long weekend and can't settle on a single person with whom to share the events of the services. There was a time when that just wasn't the case, but the higher you go in ministry the lonelier it gets. When you pastor the largest church in your area, it is highly probable that many of the pastors in your city are not happy for you. Right or wrong, that's the reality. Envy, false impressions about your attitude, and misconceptions regarding your needs by other church leaders all contribute to or cause feelings of isolation. This is one of the unfortunate realities that aspiring megachurch pastors must realize, and it's not as easy to deal with as you may think.

I often say that pastoring is the only occupation in the world where you can't admit you want to be number one. I counsel many of the professional athletes and coaches here in Cleveland and though they love God, love me, and our church, they still tell me all the time, "Pastor, I want to win it all!" They want to be number one at what they do. They want to win the championship. Being a frustrated athlete myself and loving sports, especially basketball, I grew up competing athletically all my life and I bring that same passion to what I do now. What law firm wouldn't want to be the largest in the city? What bakery wouldn't want to sell the most cakes? What printer wouldn't want to publish the most flyers? Or what business period for that matter, would not want to be the best in the area at what they do?

It is only in ministry that if one flat out says they want to be the best at what they do, it sounds like they are not saved or something, right? Or maybe, a little less extreme perhaps, they have ill, self-serving intentions? Why can't pastors whose churches are not growing just honestly say, "I want a big church!"? Just say it, God knows it anyway! Don't justify being small by condemning large or megachurches or even worse, by making statements that suggest you have no desire to be one of those "big churches."

I enjoy having a megachurch, even with all the headaches that come with it. Souls are being saved by the thousands each year because of what God is doing through us—I like that! We spend millions of dollars on our philanthropic ventures for the city of Cleveland and beyond—I like that! My family's needs are met—I like that! These are direct benefits of leading a megachurch and I thank God everyday that He picked me to do it. There is nothing wrong with wanting to be mega when your heart is in the right place.

At the same time, being the leader of a megachurch can be insufferably lonely. I preach to thousands of people each weekend at multiple services and locations, but when church is over they don't go home with me. Every Sunday night I wrestle with something I call a Sunday low. Because I've been so high off the spirit and energy of our services all weekend, Sunday evenings can be a bit of a drag. Few feelings, and I mean very few, can compare to the rush I get when souls get saved and lives are transformed because the Word went over well. It is an extremely gratifying and rewarding experience when the anointing of the Holy Spirit saturates the house and transcends all kinds of sinful barriers to accomplish the will of God.

Loneliness is a predictable Sunday evening companion who habitually and patiently waits for me to get done with all the preaching, loving, touching, crying, hugging, smiling, laughing, eating, and resting, and then decides to join me. He sometimes reminds me of things I could have said better and important things I inadvertently omitted from my message, but more often, when I think of all the great things that happened during the services, he informs me that he's really the only one who can relate.

I wish I could tell you that I've found a cure for it, but I have not. With this kind of ministry, you need an outlet, movies, sports, books— any sort of leveling mechanism that will keep you from sulking into a depression once church is over for the weekend.

I have a wife that I am madly in love with, and I can say from my heart that we are blessed from the bedroom to the bank account, but as all pastors know, sometimes you want to share your victories in ministry with another pastor. When you are the megachurch pastor in your city, whom do you call? It's hard to call a pastor who is barely making it and tell him or her how excited you are that 90 people joined your church this weekend when 90 people will not join his or her church all year.

Who do you call and talk to about how fired up you are because you are averaging a six-figure offering each weekend in the middle of a recession, when the average pastor can't fathom that kind of offering in a booming economy? You worry that if you do share your accomplishments in ministry with others who cannot identify, you'll come across as narcissistic or boastful, thus you don't talk to anyone about what God is doing in your church to avoid this characterization. It's not that you are bragging when you describe your achievements; you know God did it and have no intention of taking credit for His work. But the reality is He used you to do it, you feel good about it, and you want to share it with another pastor.

This is why most megachurch pastors end up forming friendships with megachurch pastors in other areas. Your commonality with them forges a bunker mentality that you cannot get with pastors in your city, unless you happen to be in a fairly large city that is fortunate enough to have more than one megachurch in it, and even then, you can't be friends with everybody.

When there is pressure and attention from the media of your city, if anything negative happens with you or the church, no one feels sorry for you as the guy at the top. The sad truth is that most pastors wish you would go away so things can get back to normal in the city. You are a constant reminder of a level 99% of them will never attain. You're on TV, billboards, the airwaves, and flyers that are being circulated throughout the city. Your influence is apparent and many of them secretly (and sometimes openly) yearn for something to happen that causes your influence to deflate and your appeal to decrease, so that there is less pressure for them to have to challenge themselves in their ministries. I believe the colloquial term for this is 'hating.'

Every good thing in life comes with some sacrifice. If you are going to reach this level be prepared to be alone, and unfortunately, lonely. You have to guard your anointing, keep your integrity intact, and be conscientious of your character, or the perception thereof, at all times. Consequently, as I mentioned earlier, you can't be friends with everyone anyway.

In other words, let's just say there are other pastors in your city who respect you, admire your ministry, and have nothing but positive things to say about you. That doesn't necessarily mean you can be buddies. Number one, they still can't experientially relate to your situation and two, their morals, values, principles, and code of ethics still need to align with yours in order for the two of you to have any kind of meaningful connection, which in my experience, many times, they don't. The last thing you want or need is to have your integrity compromised because people associate you with someone in ministry who has a less-than-stellar reputation. The only way you can build authentic, sustainable friendships in ministry is by being true to who you are and who God has called you to be. Prayerfully wait for Him to bless you with someone you can call a friend. In the interim, implore God to comfort you during the lonely stints. Thousands look to you to be an exemplary figure. Protect your ministry and anointing by coming to grips with the fact that you will be lonely sometimes.

PRIVACY AND SAFETY ISSUES

Megachurch pastors, especially those of us on television, basically have no anonymity. Everyone you walk by in the mall or the grocery store knows who you are. You can't take your spouse out to eat anywhere in your city without being interrupted by somebody who wants prayer, a hug, or yes, even your autograph at times. You can't just throw something on and run out to the store. People know who you are and expect you to look a certain way all the time. In the Cleveland area, I fully anticipate and have accepted the reality that every place I go, someone is going to stop me or call my name.

I don't mind the interruptions for the most part because I love people and this is the life I have chosen or rather it chose me; however, like anyone, sometimes I just want to walk in a movie theater, sit down and enjoy the movie without wondering who is looking at me or waiting for the movie to end so they can approach me.

Remember pastors, once everyone knows your name and face, there is tremendous pressure to maintain your integrity. Obviously, if you chose pastoring as a profession (or any other position of public service as we can tell from the fallout that follows when politicians commit moral failures), you know that living a life of ethical uprightness is not only expected, but also required if you want to preserve the esteem your contemporaries, constituents, or congregants have for you. Fair or not, you can't mess up. There are certain things you just can't ever do when you carry the responsibility of being a role model to thousands. If you do happen to commit certain unmentionable indiscretions, you must be prepared to deal with the consequences that come with the subjectivity of public opinion.

Your character is the crux of your ministry's capacity to mature. Have you ever considered that the reason your church is not growing, as gifted as you are, is because God is waiting for your character to catch up with your gifting? At this level, everything is magnified, especially your mistakes. I thank God daily that with over a decade of ministry behind me, there have never been any issues with women or money, which are usually the two most prominent vices that cause major ministries to fall.

Another factor worth mentioning is safety. It seems that the incidence of crazy people around you increases in direct correlation with your popularity. When you preach to thousands in the sanctuary and millions by television, you have no idea who is watching and what mental or emotional issues they might have. A couple times a year someone will call the church and say, "Tell Pastor Vernon I'm coming up there to kill him."

Certainly we have professional armed security, but if someone is intent on hurting you, ultimately only God can prevent it. As a husband and father I have to make sure that there is armed security on my wife and children at all times. My kids are in another building on our campus used for children's and teen church. I cannot take the chance of leaving them uncovered. Our home has absolutely the best alarm system we can afford and my number one assistant, who travels everywhere with me both in and out of the city, is licensed to kill. I often joke that unlike many pastors with an entourage, I have just one man with a gun.

The purpose of my transparency is not to boast in any way, nor to dissuade pastors from pursuing the lofty goal of becoming a megachurch. My point is to paint an accurate picture of the position of the megachurch pastor and to address some of the unknown truths and realities that I have not seen addressed in any of the many books I have read concerning the megachurch.

One last point I would like for you to consider in this chapter is that though most megachurches have the same basic universal issues in handling growth, there is a distinction between the Black Megachurch and other megachurches. I am writing this through the lenses of a black pastor in a poor city primarily dealing with poor black people. The Black Megachurch has to deal with all the issues I mentioned in this chapter. Those issues are often exacerbated by the pressing social and economical concerns of the black community, which you also have to address if you are serious about helping the impoverished and destitute. Though there are many white and Latino families in our church who I love and value, our demographic reflects a primarily black megachurch.

I consider myself fortunate to be in the one percent of pastors in this nation with over ten thousand members. My prayer is that the pragmatic principles of church growth I will discuss in the following chapters will help all pastors called by God to reach their maximum growth potential. Whether that number is 100 or 10,000 is ultimately up to God.

CHAPTER TWO

/ THEOLOGICAL RATIONALE FOR WHY YOU SHOULD WANT TO BE MEGA /

I'm going to be completely transparent at the onset of this chapter so you have an idea of what to expect. Throughout most of this book, I present ideas and concepts that are applicable irrespective of your theological, cultural, or social background. This chapter, however, is presented with a slightly Afrocentric slant. Why? Because I was inspired to write this chapter in particular during a specific phase in preparation for my doctorate degree, which is in Black Church studies. I learned so much during that time that has helped me to concretize my call that I feel a heightened sense of responsibility to share it with you, in hopes that what I share, if not directly germane to you, will provoke you to want to extensively explore your own call.

The religious, theoretical foundation of this book (chiefly this chapter) is grounded in a liberation theology of church growth, and in some places, black liberation theology. The centrality of liberation to the goal of becoming mega could not possibly be overstated, if you ascribe to the belief that Jesus, if He were here on earth, would be on the side of the oppressed. Without considering the liberation theology perspective, the theological posture of church growth is reduced to numbers for numbers' sake. The question that megachurch leaders (in the Black Megachurch in particular) have to ask themselves is, "What do large numbers, both in offerings and attendance, have to do with the existential conditions of hurting people in its community and city as a whole?"

The traditional approach to defining theology has generally been to begin with an etymological investigation of the word 'theology.' The rendition has gone something like this: as a compound word of Greek origin, *theos* has been defined as the divine or God, and *logos* as words or thoughts about God.[4] Until the mid-1960s, theology was only presented from a Eurocentric perspective. According to Dr. James Cone, "Unfortunately, white American theology has not been involved in the struggle for black liberation. It has basically been a theology of the white oppressor, giving religious sanction to the genocide of Amerindians and the enslavement of Africans."[5]

Cone, who is viewed by many as the progenitor of black theology, challenged the conscious of not just whites, but all those who had viewed theology exclusively through a Eurocentric lens. He was a polemical figure and was and is an unyielding apologist for the need for an Afrocentric perspective of the Bible. Cone could relate and articulate this posture academically and scholarly, but also experientially having suffered tremendous injustices personally as a black man, coupled with witnessing firsthand a nation in turmoil during the civil rights struggle.

Cone could not reconcile how what his white professors had taught him about God reflected the struggle of black people from the Trans-Atlantic Slave Trade to the present oppression of the dominant culture toward blacks in the 1960s in which he lived. *Where was God*

---

4. Duncan, Carol, Juan Floyd-Thomas, Stacey Floyd-Thomas, Stephen Ray, and Nancy Lynne Westfield, Black Church Studies: An Introduction, (New York: Abingdon Press, 2007), 74.
5. Cone, James, A Black Theology of Liberation, (Maryknoll: Orbis, 2010), 4.

in all this? Cone wondered, and at the same time had no theological construct to explicate it. Cone's mounting frustration culminated with him yelling out during one of his professor's lectures, accusing him of being a racist because nothing in his lecture addressed the existential struggle of blacks in America.

Cone's manifesto, *Black Theology and Black Power,* was both a theological and personal expression of the frustration he experienced. Though Cone respected certain perspectives of Eurocentric scholarship, he eventually created an Afrocentric perspective of theology that had never been interpreted from an academic and scholarly perspective. Cone says regarding the great European scholars:

> *Barth was useful because of his central focus on the Bible and Jesus Christ, Tillich for his focus on culture and the human situation, Bultmann for his emphasis on preaching and the present existential situation, and Bonhoeffer for his concern with the concreteness of theology as defined by the ethical demands of politics. They were like a smorgasbord of theologies from which I took what I wanted and left the rest, with Jesus Christ as my central theological norm. At no point did a European theologian, not even Barth, control what I said about the Gospel and the black struggle for freedom.[6]*

Previous to what I believe was a revelation and confirmation of his call, Cone had only been exposed to European scholarship and took some criticism from other black scholars, including his own brother, for his reliance on those white sources to articulate a black theology.

Cone seems to mirror the feeling of W.E B. DuBois who said:

> *It is a peculiar sensation, this double-consciousness, this sense of always looking at one's self through the eyes of others...One*

---

6. Cone, James, My Soul Looks Back, (Nashville: Abingdon, 1982), 83

ever feels his twoness—an American, a Negro; two souls, two thoughts, two unreconciled strivings; two warring ideals in one dark body, whose dogged strength alone keeps it from being torn asunder.[7]

Like Cone, I believe the black megachurch pastor must deal with liberation and what it has to do with the Black Megachurch. God is always on the side of the oppressed and the issue at hand is ascertaining how the megachurch can become more like Christ in its attempt to emancipate individuals who are mentally bound because of a lack of education, mentoring, assistance, and all that goes into the process of liberation.

In the last 5 years, our ministry has spent over $100,000 investing in my education and dozens of others on our staff and in our leadership tiers. The depth of my preaching is evident and it has challenged hundreds in our church to pursue higher education. Following in the tradition of the historic A.M.E. denomination, our church has now made education a prerequisite for licensing and ordination.

Understanding the arduous economic times in which we live, it is important to identify organizations that are willing to help well-meaning, called men and women of God with the ever-growing tuition costs of most accredited academic institutions. What if a person wants to be seminary trained but just can't afford it? The Black Megachurch not only has the resources but the responsibility to support academic institutions like the McCreary Center for African American Religious Studies in Cleveland, Ohio. Megachurches in general need to show their support and respect for education by establishing scholarship funds for both theological and secular instruction.

The resources and sizeable facilities of our church allow me to extend opportunities to local community colleges to open satellite

---

7. Dubois, W.E.B., Souls of Black Folk, (New York: Random House), 3.

locations on our campus. The convenience of college courses on our campus motivates our adults to go back to school and informs our young people of the necessity of preparing for their future. We also offer GED courses for individuals who have not earned their high school diplomas and all sorts of mentoring programs for those in our church and community.

The megachurch has a wonderful and unique opportunity to minister to the masses in a way that the average church cannot. In addition, the megachurch has a biblical obligation to have the heart of Christ and embrace the challenge of meeting broken people where they are on a daily basis.

> Most critics of the megachurch do not have enough information to properly critique it. The initial and immediate challenge faced by churches that grow to mega proportions seemingly overnight is threefold: First, they must devise a plan on how to nurture, disciple, and mature hundreds of inexperienced Christians; second, they must find building space to handle the influx of new people; and finally, they have to adequately address the pressing, personal needs of a congregation in the thousands. These needs create situations that require megachurches to spend a great deal of time and energy cultivating the internal growth of their members. All congregations must address their internal needs, but this has to be balanced with a reciprocal, external, contextual focus whether the church is large or small. It has taken time for the megachurch to learn this balance.[8]

For the most part, all megachurches have the same challenges of growth regardless of denomination or ethnicity. However, in addition to the ongoing struggles that come with exponential growth, the Black

---

8. Thumma, Scott, and Dave Travis. 2007. Beyond Megachurch Myths: What We Can Learn From America's Largest Churches, (San Francisco: Jossey-Bass, 2007), 78-79.

Megachurch has the added pressure of dealing with the existential needs of the black community on a daily basis. The Black Megachurch vis-à-vis other megachurches is looked to not only for spiritual guidance but also to be a major voice in the black community and a participant in the areas of education, outreach, and social justice.

In their book *From Meetinghouse to Megachurch: A Material and Cultural History*, Anne C. Loveland and Otis B. Wheeler say this:

> Historically, the Black Church served as "the spiritual, emotional, cultural, political, educational, economic, and intellectual center of the community," and many black megachurches assumed that role. If the white megachurch functioned for many of its members as a kind of oasis, the Black Megachurch constituted more of a fountainhead, the source of economic, social, and spiritual renewal in the community at large as well as in the congregational community.[9]

There is such an amalgamation of needs in the black community, especially in the area of outreach that the Black Megachurch is often overwhelmed with requests. The assumption from the black community is that the megachurch should do more than the average church to meet their needs because of its abundance of resources. Anthony Pinn says, "There is no doubt that these churches have the financial resources and personnel necessary to do good work with respect to socioeconomic and political issues. And many have programs going on for so many hours of the day that they are referred to as "seven-day-a-week churches."[10]

Pinn is dead on about the megachurch being open seven days a week. Between our multiple weekend and weekly services, business hours, for-profit ventures, outreach programs, and sports activities,

---

9. Loveland, Anne and Otis B. Wheeler, From Meetinghouse To Megachurch: A Material And Cultural History, (Columbia: University of Missouri Press, 2003), 189.
10. Pinn, Anthony B, The Black Church in the Post-Civil Rights Era. (Maryknoll: Orbis Books, 2002), 137.

the building gets a very limited amount of down time, which of course leads to steep utilities and maintenance costs. Even so, I wouldn't change a thing. It is my belief that the megachurch should do whatever it can to help both its members and the city where it is geographically located.

God placed our church in Cleveland, a city by no means known for its multiplicity of megachurches. My research concludes that we are the only black church in the Cleveland area that averages over 3,000 or more in attendance each weekend. As the senior pastor, I often wonder what God's purpose was for giving us such exponential growth and resources in a city nationally known for its economic struggles. The most obvious answer is to help liberate the least, the lost, and the left out in the Cleveland area.

Many megachurch pastors use the word 'international' in their name to suggest their impact across the world, ministries like World Changers International in Atlanta, Georgia, founded by Creflo Dollar. The idea is that they have enough people power and resources to influence not only their city, but to touch and help people across the world.

Like every church regardless of its size, each individual mega-church must concretize its assignment. Dollar pastors in a city that has dozens of megachurches, and until this recent economic downturn was the destination of many blacks across the nation looking to relocate in search of employment and a better future for themselves and their families. Because of the wealth of the city, Dollar had the luxury of focusing his resources internationally because the city he is in was prospering and had plenty of growing businesses and megachurches. Cleveland on the other hand, is not such a city. We are an urban metropolis burdened with poverty and struggle.

Living here for pretty much the entire forty years of my life, I know my city and its growing needs. Unlike Dollar and many other megachurches that use the word 'international' in their name, we consider ourselves a local church. As a matter-of-fact, we affectionately call ourselves "the city's" church. We feel the needs of Cleveland and Northeast Ohio are so great that it requires us to focus all of our time and resources locally. Last year I even wrestled with whether or not to remain on national television once I substantiated my call to the Greater Cleveland area. How could I justify being on national television when I am not called to the nation? I felt those resources could be used provincially.

My media director and my chief financial officer convinced me to stay on when they showed me that we were actually making money, not losing it, by being on national TV. Our product sales combined with people supporting us through giving (which we do not solicit), was showing a net profit for our ministry and actually helping with the overarching goal of outreach.

Cleveland needs help. The school system is suffering terribly and has been for decades now. We partnered with the CEO of the Cleveland Metropolitan School District with the hope of lifting the morale of the students. We have availed our skating rink at no cost to the district for field trips for students who are excelling academically. Because we come on local television Monday through Friday in our area, it afforded me the opportunity to allow the superintendant to be a guest on our broadcast for an entire week and share his vision and expectations for the upcoming school year with our viewing audience. I meet with the mayor regularly to discuss ways to use our influence as a church to host citywide events that are substantive to the health and growth of the area.

One such event is The Midnight Rumble, an event for men in the Cleveland area. The purpose of the event is to get young men off the street for a night and into a positive godly atmosphere. I wish I could boast that thousands of men come every year because they love my preaching and me, but the truth is they come because we offer over $10,000 in cash prizes that night. We revolve the night around basketball and flag football contests where the winning teams get $5,000 apiece in cash. Here is the catch: in order to play in the tournaments you must attend the service first.

Each year thousands of men, young and old, fill our church to capacity and hundreds flood the altar for salvation and prayer. This is possible because we have a facility that has two indoor football fields and three full-court, hardwood, regulation basketball courts, along with the necessary resources to market the event heavily on secular television and radio, and also the ability to give away $10,000.

The megachurch is a powerful force when it understands its duty and call to serve. The chief of police said that the night we had The Midnight Rumble there were virtually no crimes committed in the Cleveland area. I would like to believe that it was at least in part due to the impact of our citywide event for men. For me, hosting events like The Midnight Rumble is the megachurch serving its purpose for being mega. The Christian church is that community of persons who "got the hint," and they thus refuse to be content with human pain and suffering.[11]

As a black megachurch placed in a city deprived in so many ways, we "got the hint." Our call is to use the resources and people power afforded to us by the grace of God to help the less fortunate regardless of class or color. We are seeing more and more white and Latino families coming to us for assistance. In her book *Where We Stand: Class Matters*, bell hooks speaks to the issue of poverty being more than a black issue in America. Hooks says:

More and more Americans of all colors are entering the ranks of

---

11. Cone, James H., A Black Theology of Liberation, (Maryknoll: Orbis Books, 2010), 129.

the poor, and that includes white Americans. The evidence is in the numbers. In the essay "Trash-O-Nomics," Doug Henwood states what should be obvious but often is not: "Of course, the average white person is better off than the average non-white person, those of Asian origin excepted, and black people are disproportionally poor. But that sort of formula hides as much as it reveals: most officially poor people are white, and these days, a white household should consider itself lucky if its income is only stagnant rather than in outright decline."[12]

Outreach is what we do at "THE WORD", no matter what else we do, and we do a lot. Helping the disadvantaged people in the Greater Cleveland area is our purpose for existence. Dr. Rick Warren says, "I cannot overemphasize the importance of defining your church's purpose. It is not merely a target that you aim for; it is your congregation's reason for being."[13]

What is the Black Megachurch's role in the area of social justice? That question only became a reality to me when I began matriculating through the Black Church Studies program at Ashland Theological Seminary under the tutelage of Dr. William Myers, Professor of New Testament and Black Church Studies and also Founder and CEO of the McCreary Center for African-American Religious Studies in Cleveland, Ohio.

I will never forget the first day I walked in his office inquiring about seminary training. At the time, our church was already mega and still experiencing dynamic growth. He asked what I wanted to major in. My naïve response was, "I don't want to major in that black stuff!" Five years and two degrees later "in that black stuff," I have grown to understand both my role and the Black Megachurch's

---

12. hooks, bell, Where We Stand: Class Matters, (New York: Rutledge, 2000), 116.
13. Warren, Rick, The Purpose-Driven Church, (Grand Rapids: Zondervan, 1995), 109.

responsibility in the area of liberation, inclusive of social justice issues in our community and the world. My voice means too much and our church has too much influence not to comfort the afflicted and afflict the comfortable. Cone says:

> In the New Testament, the church (ecclesia) is the community that has received the Holy Spirit and is now ready to do what is necessary to live out the Gospel. It is the assembly of those who have become heirs of the promises of God; and because they have experienced what that means for humanity, they cannot accept the world as they know it. They must rebel against evil so all citizens may know that they do not have to behave according to unjust societal laws.[14]

If outreach is our strength then social justice is our weakness. One of the greatest challenges for me personally is finding my voice politically and in the area of social justice issues. Being raised in the 1970s and 1980s I did not experience the overt racism that Cone and other great black scholars from that era and before experienced. Coupled with that is the megachurch's appeal to various ethnicities, including a great deal of whites, which may cause many of us young, black megachurch pastors to cautiously address social justice crises, if and when at all. Our reticence to boldly engage political issues based on our reluctance to cause offense lends credence to DuBois' "double consciousness" theory. Because of the growing number of whites frequenting the megachurch and our desire to make everyone feel comfortable and accepted, many would argue that we have failed miserably in this area. Pinn says:

> It also remains to be seen if the megachurch phenomenon will enhance black Christians' abilities to influence broad political and economic issues that affect more than a small geographic

---

14. Cone, James, My Soul Looks Back, (Maryknoll: Orbis, 1986), 130.

area. Indeed, the gospel of prosperity that is preached in many of the more sizable churches may serve to hamper this national thrust. There is a tendency right now among black church men to be at ease in Zion, to kind of feel that everything is okay in the area of race and social justice, and to concentrate primarily on building our buildings and preaching success to our people. This prosperity thrust is much softer on controversial issues and tends to amplify the individual growth over national consciousness.[15]

I wholeheartedly agree with Pinn in his assessment of the mega-church at large. We are still trying to find our voice as it relates to liberation with notable exceptions like Dr. Jeremiah Wright and his successor, Pastor Otis Moss III, of Trinity United Church of Christ in Chicago. Other notable exceptions are James Meeks, who pastors the Salem Baptist Church also in Chicago, Dr. Freddie Haynes of Friendship Baptist Church in Dallas, and many other megachurches that are large, prophetic in their preaching style, politically outspoken, and unapologetically black. Though my preaching is not as political and prophetic as the aforementioned megachurch pastors because of a difference of call and assignment, I pray that "THE WORD" CHURCH is favorably changing the quality of life of hurting people in the Cleveland area both spiritually and existentially. You should consider adopting the same prayer for your organization.

---

15. Pinn, Anthony, B., The Black Church In The Post-Civil Rights Era, (Maryknoll: Orbis Books, 2002), 138.

CHAPTER THREE

/ FACILITIES /

I started "THE WORD" CHURCH in John F. Kennedy High School in Cleveland, Ohio. While I did not know it then, I believe the decision to start in a school auditorium as opposed to purchasing or renting a building was crucial to our future success. The high school offered us something that no building we could afford at the time could—room to grow. In one year, we went from about one hundred to over seven hundred in attendance each Sunday. If we had made the mistake of purchasing or leasing a storefront, I am convinced it would have dwarfed our growth.

Right or wrong, there are a lot of people who will not visit a storefront church. In their minds it speaks to failure or a lack of growth. Because most public schools have an auditorium large enough to accommodate the entire student body, they tend to seat anywhere from 500 to 2,000 people comfortably. When a visitor walks in, they see a huge facility that reminds them of the large churches they see on television with high ceilings, ample parking, and classroom space for their children. Though the congregation is small in number, the space suggests that you plan on growing. People like winners, or at least a winning attitude. Your facility says a lot about your personality. From day one, I knew that God was doing something exceptional with "THE WORD" CHURCH and sensed that we were going to experience unusual growth.

I remember that first day vividly. The atmosphere was organic and pure; people were looking for something different from what churches traditionally offered and came openhearted and openminded. I was ready and willing to deliver. I knew I would need a facility large enough to accommodate the foreseeable growth we would soon experience.

Schools give you two things that are essential to a young growing ministry: affordability and space. If you are considering starting a church in your area or if you have completely outgrown your present facility but are not quite sure if or what size you should build, I strongly suggest that you consider a local school in your area.

We started in a high school in 2000. Today, though we own a 260,000 square-feet campus that I'll discuss later, we still have several satellite churches located in high schools because of our past success.

THE PROCESS FOR RENTING AND USING
A SCHOOL FOR WORSHIP

1. Choose a school in the area you feel called to that most people in the city are familiar with and can locate easily (preferably on a main street). Make sure it has an auditorium or cafeteria conducive to worship and growth, and that it has ample parking. Plenty of parking space is a must.

2. Schedule a meeting with the superintendent or CEO of the school system, not the principal of the school. I never like to meet with people who don't have the final authority. In most cases, if the superintendent says yes, no one else can tell you no. When you meet,

share your heart and vision to spiritually and existentially help both that particular school and the city as a whole.

3. Once the superintendent and/or governing body approves your request, be sure to get at least a one-year contract. Never have your ministry held hostage by a week-to-week agreement. We have been fortunate enough in our recent school ventures to enter into contractual agreements in which we make initial investments for equipment such as sound systems, screens on the walls, etc., and whatever the initial investment price comes to, that amount is deducted from our rent so that we are often there two to three years before paying anything. The school benefits because their auditorium is updated with modern sound and video equipment that will remain even after our lease is up. We benefit because we are operating and receiving offerings in a facility with basically no overhead. The only costs we really incur are those associated with purchasing equipment, which we would have incurred regardless of where we went.

THE PROBLEMS WITH RENTING A SCHOOL

There is an old secular song by Billie Holiday, "God Bless the Child that Got His Own." Well, I'm not sure what Ms. Holiday had in mind when she wrote that song, but certainly its premise is relevant to churches.

When you're in a school, be prepared at any moment for the school to demand use of the facility at their discretion. There have been times when we had services scheduled, but had to postpone, cancel, or shift them to another location because the school had a program scheduled. The school determines what goes on when, so they can override your service times. In your contract, make sure you require a certain amount of notice in the event your service has to be cancelled so you can make the proper adjustments.

Another thing you need to be aware of is the fact that in most cases, you cannot do funerals, baptisms, or weddings in schools, for obvious reasons. But don't let that be a deal-breaker. I am a nontraditional pastor. When we needed a place to baptize, we baptized in a lake. Jesus did, didn't He? Follow the biblical example, go to your local beach if the weather permits, and take your baptismal candidates underwater. People thought we were doing something fascinating, but in all actuality, we were just being resourceful and doing what we had to do because we didn't have many other options.

If it's not the season for baptizing outside, or if you happen to be considering starting a ministry in Barrow, Alaska, check with your local YMCA or recreation center to see if there are options for renting the indoor pool. When you don't have your own, you've got to be creative. And thankfully, you've got my track record here, so just take me up on some of these suggestions if you can't think of anything on your own.

BE SURE THAT THE SCHOOL HAS
AIR CONDITIONING AND HEAT

While this may sound simple, being in a stuffy, unventilated auditorium with 500 people can be very uncomfortable. Before you set a meeting to discuss the possibility of renting a school with any board of education, find out if the school has air conditioning and heat, and, when they turn it on. Even though some schools have air, they may not turn it on until later in the summer, or later in the winter. You need to be aware of this so that you can make an informed decision regarding whether or not that's the best location for you.

Consider the average temperature in your area, but I can almost say with complete confidence that no matter what the climate, you need to have service in a ventilated room. A building that is too hot or too cold may discourage people from attending. No one wants to be uncomfortable if they can help it, especially not for an extended period of time.

DO A LITTLE HOUSEKEEPING

For the most part, the school will not be all that interested in your church, so you have to make sure it's clean and set up for your services yourself. And remember, although it's not yours, you have to take care of it like it is. You're using someone else's stuff, and you want to keep using it for awhile because holding services there is buying you time till you decide what you're going to do next. You may even need to designate a person or two for ensuring that the restrooms, children's areas, and general worship areas are clean. Trust me; an aesthetically appealing, freshly cleaned environment is worth the investment and the sacrifice.

Typically, schools have janitors that are responsible for keeping the facility clean, but don't bank on that. Janitors may not show up, or may not even be required to work or stay the entire time your services are held. Have your own staff in place to ensure the facility is clean and tidy.

AND SPEAKING OF JANITORS...

Make him your best friend. Take him to dinner, buy him some Starbucks, sow something into his life, smile at him, hug him, be nice to him. In my experience, I have found that head janitors have a lot of autonomy over the day-to-day decisions of the school. If he likes you, and you treat him well, he won't mind going above and beyond what the contract says he's required to do. So for example, if you do need him to stay a little later, unlock another door, or come at an unusual time, he'll be a lot more inclined to oblige.

DON'T LOCK YOURSELF IN

In terms of your main location, the hub or central place worshippers assemble, the absolute worst mistake any church can make is landlocking yourself. Your main location should have the potential to expand. The one thing God is not making any more of is land. If you plan to build, buy the land first; I would say a minimum of 20 acres. It's not a bad idea to purchase land before you're even ready to build if you find a great location, the price is right, and you've carefully considered the pros and cons. Give yourself room to grow. Envision your ministry with apartments, dry cleaners, restaurants, grocery stores, a spa—a city within a city.

If possible, try to locate a facility that has multiple ways to exit. If there is only one way in and one way out, traffic can and will be awful if you have back-to-back services or a major event. Can you imagine a Wal-Mart being on a side street? Position yourself as the city's church, easily accessible and customer friendly. That's why high schools are great. Most of the time, they have several ways of entering and exiting, making getting in and getting out a breeze.

Schools, banquet halls, movie theaters, or any large facility with low rent, ample space, and plentiful parking give you time to see what God is going to do before you get stuck in a building not suited to meet your long-term needs. You do not need a church building to have a great church. You just need people. Dr. Rick Warren, who started Saddleback Church in Saddleback, California says this regarding facilities and places to worship:

> Saddleback has experienced continuous growing pains throughout its brief history. To accommodate our continuous growth we used seventy-nine different facilities in the first fifteen years of Saddleback's history. Each time we'd outgrow a building, we'd move that program or service somewhere else. We often said that Saddleback was the church you could attend—if you could find us. We used four different high schools, numerous elementary schools, bank buildings, recreation centers, theaters, community centers, restaurants, large homes, professional office buildings, and stadiums, until finally we erected a 2,300-seat

high-tech tent. We were filling the tent for four services each weekend before we built our first building. I feel that most churches build too soon and too small. The shoe must never tell the foot how big it can grow.[16]

TO BUILD OR NOT TO BUILD

I personally do not believe in building when you can purchase an existing facility and design it the way you want. There is so much involved in building from the ground—hidden money that goes into digging, pouring, underground piping, and on and on. My philosophy is to buy it big and make it pretty later. Our main location was a sports facility when we purchased it. It was a place where people came to play soccer, indoor football, ice hockey and all sorts of sporting events were held there. I needed space for a growing church and it was perfect. We took one of the soccer fields and made it our sanctuary. From there we slowly and systematically remodeled and renovated as the needs occurred. When you are growing and expecting to grow more, space is everything. So many pastors limit their growth with a lack of parking, and/or limited or no space for children, both of which are highly important to visitors with small kids.

Because of my call and commitment to outreach, I am hesitant to invest the 20 to 50 million dollars it would take to build a facility equivalent to my existing space just to say I have a new building. Many churches, megachurches included, are so strapped with high mortgage payments and facility costs that it limits and oftentimes eliminates their ability to help the hurting or do substantial outreach in their community.

I am not saying I will never build a new building nor am I contending that building is a bad thing. Every pastor must know his or her assignment and be true to that. There are instances when building

---

16. Warren, Rick, The Purpose-Driven Church, (Grand Rapids: Zondervan, 1995), 45-46.

might be God's will for your ministry and the most economical way to expand your vision.

The critical point is simply this: do not let facilities limit your vision. Avoid jumping into building projects or long-term leases you will regret. Get a barometer of how fast or slow you are growing and make smart, tactical moves that will posture your ministry for success in years to come. Later, in the chapter on finance, I will talk about the importance of watching your debt and how moving too quickly can have a lasting impact on both you and your ministry.

One of the mantras I adopted several years ago after reading Steven Covey's *7 Habits of Highly Effective People*, was to begin with the end in mind. I try to follow this principle in everything I do, although, if I'm honest, I must admit because of my spontaneous personality, there are times when I don't. Almost every time I don't begin with the end in mind however, I regret it. You have to visualize where you want to be, even if you don't know exactly how you're going to get there. Covey says it this way:

> *If you want to have a successful enterprise, clearly define what you're trying to accomplish. You carefully think through the product or service you want to provide in terms of your market target, then you organize all the elements—financial, research and development, operations, marketing, personnel, physical facilities, and so on, to meet that objective. The extent to which you begin with the end in mind often determines whether or not you are able to create a successful enterprise.*[17]

Don't look at where you are now. Keep your vision in front of you and aim for it. See yourself where you want to be. Save and continue to move around, until you have enough resources to get the facility you

---

17. Covey, Stephen R., 7 Habits of Highly Effective People: Powerful Lessons in Personal Change, (New York: Simon & Schuster, 1990), 99.

need (with enough land around it to expand).

SIGNAGE

Regardless of where you hold your services, make sure you have directional signage, and no handwritten posters. Purchase or make professional, easy-to-understand signs or banners and post them throughout the facility. Large facilities need signs. The options for the shape and type of signs you can have are virtually limitless. It's probably worth it to request the services of a company that specializes in signs if you have a really big building. Their expertise will come in handy and eliminate a lot of questions you have about where you should hang them, how big they should be, etc.

DON'T MAKE YOUR MOVE TOO SOON

Later in my chapter on pitfalls to avoid, I will discuss the folly of moving too quickly, but it is important that I bring it up here because I learned the detriment of moving too quickly only after doing it. When it was obvious that we would no longer be able to remain in the high school because of our growth, we made the transition to an old movie theater in a local neighborhood. The theater hadn't been used in years, and was in need of quite a bit of work. The owners only charged me a small amount to rent it because it was in such deplorable condition. I look back now and I cringe when I think about the fact that they were only charging $2,000 a month for a facility with a huge worship space, gym, multipurpose area, and administrative offices—and at that point we were raising $40,000 a week. You do the math.

Knowing what I know now, I would have definitely waited, saved a bunch of cash, and added a few more services in a high school or something. Without question, we had definitely outgrown that location, and in order to avoid stunting our growth, I had to make some adjustments. (Not moving quickly enough can be just as problematic as moving too quickly). Retrospectively speaking, I should have kept renting our main facility and opened another location in a high school, until we had raised enough money to pay for something cash. However, having received very little education in finance and debt management, my poverty mentality and ignorance spurred me to move too quickly.

There is a great book called *The Total Money Makeover*, written by Dave Ramsey, a Christian financial analyst with a no-nonsense approach to debt and money. Dave's theory and basis for his book is "If you live like no one else, later you can live like no one else."[18] Ramsey doesn't believe in having any debt, and I just recently finished a series called, "Owe No Man Anything," based on his theory and Romans 13:8, "Owe no man anything but to love one another." Proverbs 22:7 says, "The rich rule over the poor and the borrower is slave to the lender."

The teaching in this book definitely goes against our cultural grain, and by "our" I mean Americans in general. That's pretty obvious when you consider that a staggering 90% of people in our culture buy things they can't afford.

The same is true for those of us who lead megachurches. If the plan is that we'll pay it off in 20 or 30 years, that means we've purchased something we can't afford. We'll discuss finance at length in another chapter, but the critical point is this: save, save, save, and then purchase your building with cash. Debt is debilitating, enervating, and makes you vulnerable to those who you owe, from a personal and ministry perspective. Don't borrow.

---

18. Ramsey, Dave, The Total Money Makeover: A Proven Plan for Financial Fitness, (Nashville: Thomas Nelson, 2003) 5.

CHAPTER FOUR

/ PREACHING STYLE /

Have you ever frequented a restaurant that was professional in every way? There was great parking, and then once inside you quickly noticed it had pleasing aesthetics, a courteous staff, and a great atmosphere. You were totally impressed with everything—until you tasted the food. If the food isn't delicious, no matter how great everything else is, chances are you won't be dining there again. The purpose of going to a restaurant is to eat, to be fed. If there are other great things about the restaurant, they're merely a plus.

Church is no different. People come to be fed spiritually and if your food isn't good, chances are they will look for another church with better food. Therefore, what you teach and preach is decisively important. No matter how plentiful your parking is, how kid-friendly your childcare is or how likable your staff is, people come for the food. In most cases, the determining factor of them visiting again or joining the ministry is their degree of enjoyment with the pastor's preaching style and relevance to their existential issues. Ultimately, people join a church where they look forward to hearing the message each week. Each pastor must determine what their preaching approach will be.

Training hundreds of pastors across the nation, I am humbled that so many men and women of God are impressed with our methodological approach to church growth. I am flattered when pastors share their desire to emulate the professionalism of our staff, our flow of worship and the other features of our ministry that facilitate our church's continued growth. Sadly, the one ingredient that is often overlooked by pastors is the importance of good preaching.

Let me say right away that I am an apologist for seminary training. I believe every pastor should pursue a formal theological education if possible. Seminary does not make you a preacher, but if you have been called to preach and pastor it will undoubtedly improve the substance of your preaching. Every pastor must determine what his or her style will be. I am convinced that no one style of preaching is universal. Certainly, it should be Christ-centered and cogent, however, your homiletical approach is based on who you are and the audience you want to attract. Every pastor has a specific call and crowd, which should direct his approach to preaching. You can determine your style by first clarifying your target audience.

Rick Warren says:

When I took hermeneutics and preaching classes in seminary, I was taught that to understand the message of the New Testament I had to first understand the geography, customs, culture, and religion of the people who lived at the time. I could then extract the timeless, eternal truth of God from that context. This process is called "exegesis." Every biblical preacher uses it. Unfortunately, no class taught me that before I communicate that timeless truth to people today, I need to "exegete" my own community! I must pay as much attention to the geography, customs, culture, and religious background of my community as I do to those who lived in Bible times if I am to faithfully communicate God's Word.[19]

---

19. Warren, Rick, The Purpose-Driven Church, (Grand Rapids: Zondervan, 1995), 160.

When I started "THE WORD" CHURCH, I quickly observed that those in the crowd were between the ages of 18 and 40. Many were black males who were un-churched and reared in broken homes. Right away I had a choice to make. Would I continue preaching the same way I did at my first pastorate, which was a traditional Baptist church that enjoyed the "hooping" style of preaching? Or would I make the adjustment to shape my lessons to fit the crowd I was attracting who did not really understand why the preacher would be "singing his sermon" as opposed to just talking to them about their daily struggles of faith, family, and finance?

By no means am I suggesting that hooping, or any other style of preaching for that matter, is improper. You must know your audience. There are megachurches in America where the pastor barely speaks above a whisper; conversely, there are megachurches where the preaching is loud and expressive. The 21st century pastor must be willing to adjust his presentation to the ever-expanding culture that we live in.

Adapting to the society in which we live means embracing, not rejecting, many of the ways in which our culture has changed. We are certainly more technically advanced than we were a decade ago, and this trend is likely to continue. We are more socially connected through mobile and internet technology than we have ever been before. We have far less face-to-face interaction handling our daily business considering we have self-checkout express lanes in the grocery store, ATM machines that allow us to do almost any banking transaction necessary, and computers, cell phones and electronic tablets that allow us to pay bills, shop, conduct research, send greeting cards to a relative in another country, learn a new language and check books out from the library. You name it; you can just about do it with a screen and without ever having to see another person's face.

To compete with, or perhaps a more constructive approach, to complement, the everyday conveniences your parishioners are used to, incorporate ways of showing your awareness of the benefits of technology. If and when you can afford it, put up large screens in your sanctuary so that visitors can participate in the worship service by reading the lyrics to the songs that are sung or read scriptures along with you as you give the biblical context for your sermon. They're used to watching and using screens anyway. (Do not assume they know your music or that they have a Bible with them to follow you in your message). Get a Facebook page and post pictures of your events, services, and inspirational quotes from your message. Pastors must modernize their method of preaching to reach a new generation of believers who do not have or necessarily desire "the old-time religion."

MIC CHECK

Another choice that impacted my preaching style was my preference of microphones. For years I held the mic in my hand. It was all I had ever seen the preachers I grew up watching and imitating do. Normally, in traditional black church settings, the microphone is stationary on the podium until the pastor reaches his climax. At that point many pastors will remove it from the podium and hold it in their hand. I find both ways to be restrictive and highly recommend a lapel mic that keeps your hands free. This gives you latitude to be more creative by using props, engaging the audience, and an overall feeling of freedom and comfort while preaching. It takes some getting used to but I really believe it is worth trying.

WHAT ARE YOU WEARING?

The clothes you wear say a lot about your style and who you are trying to draw. I used to wear suits that cost up to $1,000 every Sunday. One weekend while sitting in church, I noticed that most of the men in my church didn't have on suits. Whether it was because they could not afford them or because it was just not their style, I got the message. I called my leaders together and announced we would become the "Come-as-you-are church," and adapted our church motto: "Come as you are, you won't stay as you are." From that moment until now I have dressed casual during my weekend messages and Wednesday Bible studies. That is not to say that I don't occasionally wear a suit, but for the most part, I normally don a nice shirt and some jeans or dress pants. I preach in Nike jogging suits, two-piece outfits, or the latest Hip-Hop apparel. I believe in letting the series I am preaching and the season of the year dictate my dress.

I usually preach something light during the summer months. Most of my people are vacationing so that's not the time for me to do a series on my vision for the church. Many times I teach on relationships in the summer. Nothing fills up our church like series on relationships. During the warm months, when most churches experience a decline in both offerings and attendance, we are seating people in our overflow areas. People in general, but especially the young crowds I attract, are struggling with sexual identity, being grown and alone, marriage, blended family drama, and everything in between. For years, it was taboo to do a sermon series on sexuality and relationships. Out of the hundreds of series that I have preached, without a close second, our bestselling DVDs have been my material on relationships.

When it's warm outside and I'm preaching an important but fun series, I dress the part. I will often wear clothes that are comfortable and casual. In September, when my people are returning from vacations and kids are headed back to school, I dress a little more serious because I am normally in a weighty series dealing with prayer, finance, vision, etc. Very seldom do I wear a tie because that is just not who I am. I preach eight or nine services a week so being dressed comfortably is highly important to me.

At the same time, Joel Osteen, who pastors Lakewood Church in Houston, Texas, wears a dark suit and tie every Sunday. He has the largest church in America with a weekly attendance of 43,500 parishioners. Every pastor must choose a style that fits your audience (or the audience you are trying to attract) and most of all, a style that both you and your congregants are comfortable with.

WHAT THEN SHALL WE PREACH?

While your preaching style is a choice, substance is not. I believe that meaty messages are a must. So what should you preach about? I cannot overestimate the centrality of the cross. Whatever else we preach, people still need the clearly defined Gospel of Jesus Christ. But what else should we preach? One of the best books I have ever read regarding preaching is Dr. Marvin McMickle's, *Where Have All the Prophets Gone?* In his book, he challenges all clergy in the area of prophetic preaching and tells why it is important. He says:

> *Prophetic preaching shifts the focus of a congregation from what is happening to them as a local church to what is happening to them as a part of a society. Prophetic preaching then asks the question, "What is the role or the appropriate response of our congregation, our association, and our denominations to the events that are occurring within our society and throughout the world?" Prophetic preaching points out those false gods of comfort. Further, it points out a lack of concern and acquiescence in the face of evil that can so easily replace the true God of scripture who calls true believers to the active pursuit of justice and righteousness for every member of society. Prophetic preaching also never allows the community of faith to believe that participation in the rituals of religious life can ever be an adequate substitute for that form of ministry that is*

20. McMickle, Marvin, Where Have All the Prophets Gone? Reclaiming Prophetic Preaching in America. (Cleveland: Pilgrim Press, 2006), 2-3.

designed to uplift the "least of these" in our world.[20]

McMickle believes there is a paucity of courageous pastors that are willing to preach prophetically. As much as I agree with the need for prophetic preaching, I don't think pastors should be limited to it. When asked if I am a prophetic preacher, my answer is an unequivocal yes. Having the ear of thousands of people each weekend along with being on both local and national television, I agree with Finley Peter Dunne, a Chicago-born writer, that it is our responsibility to "afflict the comfortable and comfort the afflicted." Not a weekend goes by that I don't remind our church of our responsibility to the destitute of our community.

While the pulpit (or stage if you've learned a thing or two from me) can be a powerful political platform, I have neither the passion nor savvy of McMickle, but I do speak out on the relevant issues of our city and nation when necessary. I am not only a prophetic preacher, but at times I am sure I have been called a "prosperity preacher" because of my belief in the power of money in the life of the believer. I believe prosperity plus integrity equals kingdom victory.

I do not believe any pastor should be limited to one way of preaching each week. Sometimes you may be prophetic, other times you may be patriotic, and still at other times you may feel led to preach an entire series on prosperity. Regardless of what topic you cover in your message, the important thing is to be relevant. As pastors and godly leaders, we have an obligation to preach about the social and spiritual issues affecting people most.

My challenge to all pastors is to preach what God tells you your congregation needs and preach with prudence. People want to know what your sermon has to do with their particular life difficulties. The average person in my church is sitting there thinking about the bills on their table, the person they are married to or want to get married to, their past issues that are holding them hostage and all the baggage that comes with life. They are not interested in my particular theological construct regarding eschatology. In my estimation, one of the greatest keys to our success has been relevant preaching that meets people where they are.

MONEY

I don't preach a lot about tax evasion because to my knowledge, that isn't a struggle for most of the people attending my church. However, I do preach about money and if you want to increase the financial fortitude of those who you shepherd, you should too. Lack of education or improper education in finance is a major reason why people are in debt and why they can't or don't give.

The growth of your church will be severely handicapped if people are unable to give because they are encumbered by debt or because they have never been taught on the importance of giving. You can enlighten them on both matters by sharing with them how consistently and systematically paying their tithes gives the church the purchasing power to meet the needs of the membership. The more you have, the more you can do to strengthen the city and as a result, propitiously affect them as individuals and collectively as a community of people.

There is no place for diffidence in the pastorate, especially when it comes to teaching about money. If you feel insecure about preaching on finance, evaluate your motives. When you have good intentions, you can preach with confidence.

Being a seminarian, I am offended and appalled by a lot of the preaching I see on television regarding finance. In order to receive offerings or gain monetary partnership from viewers, many television preachers either massacre or apply a strained exegesis to biblical texts on finance. Don't do that. Avoid using your voice for personal gain. Stick to the scriptural mandates regarding money and deliver it with gentle diligence. Your job as the spiritual guide is to teach people the unadulterated truth of God's Word with hopes that they will receive it, apply it, live it, and share it. When they do, your ministry will grow.

HOMOSEXUALITY

I preached a message a long time ago called "When God Gives You a Friend," and it was based on the genuine friendship between David and Jonathan. I am aware of the recent efforts by homosexual advocates to interpret this relationship as something more than a purely, God-centered camaraderie, but I am not going to spend too much time here deconstructing the clear fallacy of their position.

If you are really interested in learning more about that however, read Dr. Richard Hays' book, *The Moral Vision of the New Testament*, where he deems these attempts at inserting permissible homosexuality into scripture "exegetical curiosities," that "can only be judged pathetic efforts at constructing [scriptural] warrant for homosexual practice where none exists."[21] Another great book, *When God Goes to Starbucks*, by Dr. Paul Copan, who incidentally also quotes Hays, covers this distorted attempt at homosexual justification in the Bible as well, but from an apologetics perspective.

Whether we like it or not, the prevalence of present-day proponents of homosexual privilege prescribe that we as Christians become versed in the positions of our homosexual colleagues and counterparts. I can't possibly explicate the entire argument on the matter, but read the books I just mentioned so that you are properly prepared to discuss them when necessary. Oh, and for balance, you may want to read Dr. Horace Griffin's, *Their Own Receive Them Not*. Dr. Griffin is an openly gay African-American

---

21. Hays, Richard. The Moral Vision of the New Testament, (New York: Harper Collins, 1996) 395.

professor who engages homosexuality from a black liberation theology viewpoint. You can't adequately condemn or pick apart a particular ideological construct until you understand both sides of the argument.

You can't dodge it either. The unfortunate state of our union is such that homosexuality is an acceptable lifestyle, and in many states, the law asserts that those who choose that lifestyle should be afforded the same rights, privileges, and acknowledgment that heterosexuals do. In the African-American church, generally speaking, we've been less inclined to engage homosexuality as a topic of our Sunday morning sermons. We have homophobic tendencies, in that if we address it all, we shun and rebuke the behavior (which we should for any sinful conduct), but we offer no compassion, consideration, or help for those who want to understand why their way of life is wrong, or what they can do to change.

As the moral center of the community, churches have to show love and humanity for our gay and lesbian brothers and sisters, as Christ would have. They are sinners, but no worse than the other fornicators, liars, and drug addicts in our church. We do not compromise the Word of God in any way to make them feel comfortable, but while we forthrightly address the immorality in their lives, we must neutralize our homophobia by refraining from labeling, assuming, and shaming.

PREACH IN SERIES

Preach a string of related messages and give them a single, catchy title whenever possible. Many pastors are skilled at putting one sermon together, but don't know how to preach in series. I have discovered that in order to build people, you need to preach on a particular subject over several weeks or even months. This allows for emphasis, reiteration, and repetition. Series also permit you to both challenge and develop your people in whatever you're dealing with.

One message rarely affords you enough time to properly exegete it, especially if you are dealing with any of what I call the big three: faith (prayer, purpose, biblical doctrine, etc.), family (marriage, children, singlehood, sexuality, etc.), or finance (tithes, debt, giving, etc.).

Also, preaching in series allows your staff to prepare marketing materials, stage props, musical selections, and other complementary additions to engage your audience in a more interactive, attention-grabbing manner. From the media department to the music department, everything follows my preaching. If they know in advance that I am going to be preaching something for awhile, they can create skits, props, or video presentations to go along with the message.

But, I have also discovered over the years, one of the major mistakes pastors make is staying in one series too long. Like it or not, people tend to bore quickly, so you must find a balance on how long to preach a particular theme. Four to six weekends is long enough on any series. If you feel a pull to stay longer because of the depth and wealth of information you have to impart during a particular series, I recommend doing the series in volumes. Take a break from it, preach something else, and then preach "Blah, Blah, and Blah – Volume 2" later in the year or preach the same topic but give the series a completely different title six months thereafter.

Also, in terms of series, something I realized that revolutionized our ministry is that it is essential to preach the same thing on Wednesdays. In years past, I would preach one series on weekends, and another on Wednesdays, thus I had to have two series prepared at all times. This was not only mentally taxing, but probably not the most effective use of my time. As a result, I decided to preach the same series on weekends and Wednesdays.

I know what you're thinking. Half the church doesn't come on Wednesdays. That's true in most churches, but I have found that if you do part two on Wednesday, your midweek attendance will increase. This sends a message to your crowd that you are not going to wait for those who don't come on Wednesday. I tell my congregation if they don't come on Wednesday, they'll miss half of what God has to say. Plus, I've discovered that people need congruency. You can't discuss faith on weekends, and love on Wednesdays. For those who are doing two different messages, try my suggestion. If it doesn't work for you, remember, you can always go back to doing it the way you were doing it before.

Because I'm a seminarian, I love deep exegetical teaching. But there's a place for it, and most of the time, it's not in the weekend service. I have a doctorate of ministry and can use my education to pedantically engage my audience whenever I want, but what purpose would that really serve? Sure, it's okay to challenge them, and throw in some new theories here and there to make sure you are stimulating them intellectually and spiritually, but to preach a whole sermon in some obscure manner that nobody understands but me and a few other people is antithetical to what I'm trying to accomplish. I choose to use a simplified, straightforward approach in my messages.

Most of my fellow seminarians are limiting their growth because of their profoundly complex messages. While there are a handful of people in every church that would like to hear these kinds of messages, for the most part, if you preach over the heads of your attendees by using theological terms they've never heard, and assuming their scholarship by discussing complicated theological subjects, your attendance will plummet. Save the deep stuff for your meetings with other pastors, elders, or ministers, or establish a class during the week for those who want weighty, philosophical teaching. The hardest crowd to preach to is one that is asleep and if you bore them, you'll look out in your crowd and see nodding heads and open mouths.

By no means am I suggesting that you should be shallow; you'll have to determine how heavy your messages should be by evaluating the biblical and academic competence of your members. Harmonize homiletics with hermeneutics to provoke interest and present an exciting, scripturally sound message.

The title of your messages, regardless of the content, needs to be enticing. Who wants to hear a deeply titled sermon? Use a popular movie title, a memorable song, or a hot topic. Subjects draw people. Once you reel them in you can teach them whatever you need to. You can't preach to people who aren't there and they're not coming if you don't captivate them with a catchy message title. I have even found that turning on the Hip-Hop station can be helpful. Hip-Hop is no longer my preference of music, however, it is for many of the young people who frequent my church, so in order to be relevant, I have to know what they're listening to. For you, it may not be the Hip-Hop station; it may be the local pop station. Whatever your target market is, be sure that you're in sync with their cultural preferences and norms.

Your message should be substantive but pertinent to the most pressing concerns your members have. At the end of the day, the people in your church are not seminarians. Like it or not, the average young brother that walks in is not interested in Martin Luther's Reformation or whether the effect of Constantine's third century influence was good or bad on the Judeo-Christian church. They want information that they can use in their daily lives.

I've met so many pastors that hinder their growth because of their repudiation of modern ministry methods, especially in their preaching style. One pastor told me, "I'm not going to preach that fluff stuff or use catchy titles. I am going to preach my deep subjects." I hope the 20 people that come to his church each week are getting deeper. I know pastors with great hearts and study habits, but their messages are too boring to sustain any kind of growth.

To give you an idea of what I mean, here is a list of some of the sermon and series titles I've used in the past:

- Me, Myself, and I (popular song title)

- Love, Sex, and Relationships (anytime you mention sex, people come)

- Raising Someone Else's Child (blended family issues)

- The Authority of Money (people like to have authority and money)

- Desperate Housewives (what women need from their husbands)

- I Think I Love My Wife (what men need from their wives)

- Divorce Court (what the Bible says about divorce and remarriage—we actually used our stage as a courtroom. I wore a judge's robe and we reenacted a scene from a divorce court case. Our crowd loved it!)

Clearly, these are just a few of the many sermons that I have preached, but if you're really interested in learning more about my messages/titles, you can view our catalog online at wordcity.org.

CHAPTER FIVE

/ STAFFING /

Staffing is crucial to any successful organization including the megachurch and any church experiencing exponential or even consistent growth. Every pastor should consider the task of selecting his team members as crucial as any he will ever undertake. Over the years I have gotten pretty good at it, but like most megachurch pastors whose church has exploded with growth, I have made my share of mistakes in this area and hope to help you avoid the same errors.

DO NOT MAKE YOUR MOVE TOO SOON

Most pastors make the critical mistake of hiring too quickly when their ministry begins to flourish and grow, which, from my own experiences, I totally understand. You look around one day and because of the favor of God, all of sudden you can no longer handle the load with just volunteers and the time for full-time staff has come. Because you have never been in a position that mandated you make such decisions before, and you feel as if you have no one you can trust enough to ask for help or advice, you find yourself blindly trying to figure out how to do it and end up hiring the wrong person or persons.

The first rule of hiring is not to hire prematurely. I would say the first rule is not to hire the wrong person, but sometimes, you don't discover that a person is the wrong person until a time long after you have offered them a compensation package and asked them to come on board. However, I can almost guarantee you that if you make a hiring decision in haste, it will almost always be the wrong person. Is this an absolute rule? Of course not. Sometimes, you do what you feel you have to do and it ends up working out in the end. God understands your exigency, knows your heart, and blesses you with good people, even if you did hire them without giving the decision due diligence. Certainly, in my own experience I can attest to the latter. But, I can also attest to the former. Hiring impulsively can cost both you and your ministry dearly.

It is better to leave a position vacant than hire an unsuitable candidate. Many times, pastors think they have to hire someone to prevent the ministry from falling apart. They quickly forget that the same God that gave them the growth can help them maintain it until the right person arrives or is trained to fill the position. If you are not sure what to do, don't do anything. Just wait and keep using volunteers. I have learned over the years that it is easy to get them in; it is hard to get them out. In my experience, hiring someone who wasn't the right fit precipitated their termination because they were hurting or limiting the potentiality of our ministry in some way.

If you have a pastor's heart, it is extremely difficult to take away someone's income, especially someone who is not only an employee, but also a member of your church and in some cases, even a family member. (I know a pastor who had to fire his own mother). As tough a task as firing someone you love may be, you must reconcile this reality if you come to the point where it is necessary to release him or her from your staff. As their pastor, you will love them and will be there for them always; as the CEO, you must do what is best for the future of the ministry.

Dr. Chand, conference speaker and former president of Beulah Heights Bible College in Atlanta, Georgia, deals with this in his book, Chand writes:

> I have conversations with pastors who have problems with paid staff. They have a difficult job today. On one hand, they are pastors—that means they're shepherds who care for the sheep. On the other hand, they are the Chief Executive Officers (CEOs) and the congregation holds them responsible for the smooth running business of the church. The first thing I've learned is that even though they are both pastor and CEO, they can't be both at the same time. I try to help them understand the difference between the two and when to give priority to one and when to the other. [22]

It has been my custom to give healthy severance checks to people we have to let go. I do that in cases where I feel I did not properly evaluate whether a person was the right one for the job. No, they did not work out, but I should have prayed before I invited them on staff. Integrity requires that I pay for my mistake also. Regrettably, we have had to write several such checks over the years and that has taught us the valuable lesson of hiring slowly.

THE TWO TYPES OF STAFF

There are two types of staff—paid staff and unpaid staff—but they are all staff. When you experience dynamic growth, it is not possible to hire all the people you need to run the ministry. Pastors must quickly learn and appreciate your most prized commodity—volunteers. Volunteers are free labor. Categorizing ministry servants in this way is

---

22. Chand, Samuel R., Who's Holding Your Ladder? (New York: Mall Publishing. 2003), 34-35.

not meant to diminish their value, but rather quite the opposite. These individuals unselfishly avail themselves to the ministry and are integral to the ministry's success because of the fact that they labor for free.

In the megachurch environment where there are multiple services oftentimes in several locations, it is nearly impossible to pay enough people to pull it off. You need people to help direct traffic, park cars, drive shuttle buses and vans, serve in the nursery and children's church areas, greet, usher, provide information, and handle hundreds of other responsibilities to make your church run smoothly. Clearly, you can't continue to use the same volunteers over and over again at all your locations. Each location needs its own staff to run effectively, lest you run the chance of burning out your best people.

The reality is, whether they get paid or not, they are the face of the ministry for first-time visitors. Make no mistake about it; your visitors see them as staff. Think about it. If I visit your church for the first time, how do I know who gets paid and who doesn't? All I know is that whoever is serving me represents the organization. This is actually true for those who visit often and even for those who are new members of your church as well. Unless one of my paid staff members are specifically pointed out as such for one reason or another, oftentimes parishioners are unaware of who receives a paycheck for what they do, and who is doing it for no pay at all.

The parking guy has on a jacket and hat with the church's logo on it; he represents the ministry. He is absolutely crucial to what we do and should be viewed as a part of the staff. It is critical that you continually invest in training and building your volunteers and that you reward them for their selflessness as much as possible. Remember, most people work Monday through Friday and get the weekend off. In essence, your volunteers are sacrificing one and sometimes both of their days off to make your ministry run smoothly. You should always keep that in mind as a pastor.

Once a month, we take several of our ministries to dinner. We typically rent out an entire section of a great buffet in the area. My wife and I, along with several members of our paid staff, get there early so we can eat before our buses arrive with our volunteers. Once they arrive, we spend our time working the room, going from table to table expressing our gratitude and learning as many names as we can, which is quite a task when you deal with hundreds of volunteers.

Because we have several locations, a few of our key ministry leaders often serve at one location and then drive to another. We are acutely aware of the rising cost of gas prices thus we give gas cards to those who need it and have even purchased vehicles for committed people in ministry.

We expect and demand that our volunteers maintain the same spirit of excellence and professionalism that our paid employees do. We help them understand it is a privilege that we allow them to serve in a ministry of this caliber and gain the invaluable experience that they often incorporate in their businesses and places of employment. However, we equally balance this with our expression of the high level of appreciation we have for them. Never minimize your volunteers; they are the heart of any successful, growing ministry.

THE THREE Cs

In his book *Courageous Leadership*, Bill Hybels, pastor of Willow Creek Community Church in South Barrington, Illinois, deals with the three essential characteristics of any potential staff member: character, competence, and chemistry. After 30 years of leading one of the most familiar megachurches in America and of course making his share of premature hires, Hybels says (and I have come to agree), "If you try to get around any of the three Cs you will pay for it." [23]

---

23. Hybels, Bill, Courageous Leadership, (Grand Rapids: Zondervan, 2009), 81.

CHARACTER

There is a young lady who has taken your department to another level. She is educated, proficient, dependable, and has great people skills. The problem is she has had problems in the past with being promiscuous. You knew it when you hired her but ignored it because of her talent and the fact that you felt you really needed to get someone quickly in that position. Inevitably, because she had never resolved her issues, she ends up sleeping with several married men in the church. As gifted as she is and as much as the staff liked her, she lacked character.

So many pastors, especially young, inexperienced pastors whose churches are growing much more quickly than they anticipated, make the mistake of hiring people with unproven character. I remember some years ago as our church was exploding with growth, I needed someone (or at least I thought I did) to handle the finance department for me because money was coming in fast and I had very little business or finance experience. A gentleman from another city with whom I was doing business was so impressive over the phone in the area of finance that I decided to offer him the CFO position of our ministry. I relocated his family and gave him what, at the time, was an amazing salary and benefit package, especially for such a young ministry. A bishop in our city got word that I had hired the gentleman and called me immediately. He said emphatically, "Vernon, get him out of your church. He has a history of womanizing and he's going to hurt your ministry."

By that time I had already developed a friendship with the man, had spoken with his wife and told her the move to Cleveland would be worth it for her and her children. I really wanted to honor our agreement. Not only did I relocate his family, but in my naiveté I allowed him to bring his female assistant. As predicted by the bishop who had warned me, he ended up having an affair with one of the women in our finance department and he was sleeping with the assistant he brought with him.

To this day, I consider him one of the brightest financial minds I have encountered and he got along great with our team, but he lacked character at the time and I ignored it hoping it would not affect our staff. I certainly came to regret that decision.

COMPETENCE

Whether you pastor a megachurch or a church with a couple hundred people, always hire educated and/or experienced people. Without question, the larger you get the more critical a competent staff becomes.

Let's say there is a secretary on your staff who has impeccable character and everybody on staff simply adores her. She has great chemistry with the rest of the team. There is only one problem. She can't type! As much as you and the team love her, she does not have the skill set to take you to the next level; either you can type or you can't.

First and foremost, because of her great attitude and willing heart, your first move may be to invest in additional training for her if she is willing to get better and grow with the organization. When you hired her years ago, the church was in a different place and she was adequate for that season, but unlike the ministry she did not keep progressing and her skills are no longer up to par. Either she is willing to get better or she has to go. Parishioners pay you not only to preach, but also to make the hard but necessary choices for the future success of the ministry.

In megachurches, we deal with millions of dollars in offerings. You cannot make your brother the CFO because he is kin to you. You need someone with an MBA to handle your finances. You need someone with a degree in English to write the content for your website and all your correspondence. You need great people answering your phones.

Your customer service is crucial. When I call any company chances are the CEO is not going to answer the phone, so my first impression of the company is how the person who answers the phone sounds. Does the person speak well? Did they seem flustered or under control? Did they seem prepared and ready for me as a customer? These things often separate great companies from good ones.

At this point in our ministry, I can no longer hire my family or friends because I love and trust them. I need the best. Someone from The White House may call our church; I have to know my receptionist can intelligently address them. I need the best media people; millions are watching us on television across the world. If your church has grown to the point of needing full-time staff, look for competent people. If you have already hired people who do not have the skill set to take you to the next level, challenge them to grow with the company and invest in them so that they keep up with the ministry. If they are unwilling, make the hard choice of letting them go and hire someone who has the capacity to soar with your vision for the future of your ministry. Do not compromise on competence.

CHEMISTRY

The last of the Cs is chemistry. I remember we brought a young lady on staff a few years ago. She was gifted, educated, and living for the Lord. She would come early and stay late. Any task you gave her, she would complete quickly and with excellence. I was so impressed with her effort and ability that I quickly promoted her to our executive team and welcomed her input. Suddenly, I began to notice that our team was not clicking as well and there was a bizarre feeling in our staff meetings. Something was not the same but I could not figure it out. Over the next month I began calling my staff in one at a time to try to get a sense of what was happening with the team.

The issue was that this young, gifted, addition to our staff was going from office to office planting negative seeds about our organization and how it was being managed. She was literally trying to start a mutiny because of the injustices she perceived. One person had divided our staff because of a lack of chemistry. We had no moral issues with her and she might have been the most educated and gifted person on the team, but she lacked chemistry with us. She just did not fit our culture. I suppose she meant well, but because things were not operating the way she thought they should, she incited widespread dissension that undermined the solidarity of our staff. I believe she was sincere in her actions, but she was not called to be a part of our staff. Do not minimize the importance of chemistry.

Hybel summarizes his theory of the three Cs by saying this:

I admit this without a hint of apology. One of the reasons I am having such a ball doing ministry these days is finally, after almost three decades of team building, all our major leadership teams are built according to the criteria I've been describing. Throughout our teams we have people with sky-high character, off-the-chart competence, and extraordinary chemistry. What's not to like? When I go to work each day I feel like a schoolboy going out for recess. [24]

DO NOT OVERPAY

One of the other key lessons I've learned in my staffing experience is how to compensate fairly. Early in my ministry, with little knowledge of church growth and its accompanying challenges, I often paid the recruits I hired much more generously than their position, experience, or job responsibility called for. Before I knew it, my payroll had greatly exceeded what it should have been, and the state of our finances was grossly imbalanced.

24. Hybels, Bill, Courageous Leadership, (Grand Rapids: Zondervan, 2009), 85.

I did not base their compensation on the factors that traditionally dictate what a person will be paid for doing a particular job; however, I did base it on what a job traditionally paid for a particular position. In other words, if I hired someone to work as an office manager, I would pay him or her what the median salary for an office manager was in our area, with no consideration given to their lack of commensurate job experience or education. If I believed that a person could do the job, then I paid them what I thought they should have. I am almost embarrassed to admit that there was not more science to it than that.

Retrospectively, I know that I did both them and myself a disservice. While I meant well, paying them well above what I could afford and what they deserved at the beginning of their tenure led to me having to make some unnecessarily tough decisions later on. By overpaying them, I gave them nowhere to grow financially, thus they had little aspiration to grow professionally. In addition, I put myself in a position to have to retract some of my generous efforts later on, once I became informed as to what I should have actually been paying and what our financial situation mandated I pay in order to balance our books appropriately.

Megachurches and non-megachurches alike are a bit more unpredictable than corporate sector organizations in terms of revenue. While every organization, for-profit and nonprofit, have good and bad years, the revenue stream of churches is based on so many variable factors that offerings can fluctuate up to 50% depending on the week. Thus, ensuring that you keep your payroll to a level that is comfortable is essential. Consequently, even if you do have a bad week, bad month, or even a bad year in offerings, that doesn't have to translate to your employees' paychecks.

By no means am I suggesting that you not pay equitably. On the contrary, I would encourage you to be fair and offer a few extra perks if you can. We employ the bonus system at "THE WORD" CHURCH.

I frequently stop by the various offices of my staff and bless them with bonus checks in increments of $100, $500, and even $1,000 when we have a windfall and I know that they have been giving the company all they have. If we have an especially arduous few weeks, I might give them a week off with pay. My wife and I have been blessed to have a home in a climate warmer than Cleveland; our staff (both paid and unpaid leaders) is welcome to use it whenever they want to take a vacation at no cost to them.

The worst thing in the world is to have to take money away from people. If you have ever been on the receiving end or giving end of this news, you know exactly what I mean. Once a person is accustomed to living a certain type of lifestyle that you afforded them based on what you decided to pay them, causing them to have to make adjustments can be deflating, demoralizing, and discouraging. In many cases, people do not live beneath their means and so taking money away from them can wreak havoc on their home and family life. There are so many adverse trickle-down effects spanning the gamut from financial to emotional, it is far better to just pay people what you know you can afford, and if you cannot find a person willing to do what you need for that amount, hold off from hiring until you do, or until you are in a position to pay more.

HIRE PAID STAFF FROM WITHIN

Another practice that I have begun to implement more and more is hiring from within the ministry from the pool of volunteers that have been serving for a year or more. This has proven to be one of our most favorable customs of hiring. There are a number of reasons as to why this works. You know the person before you decide to bring them on staff. They have been in your leadership meetings, you have touched them and their families, you know they have your heart and the spirit of the ministry, you have seen their leadership capacity, they have demonstrated their worth and how much they value the ministry by working for free, they understand your goals, they know your vision...need I say more?

Certainly there is nothing wrong with hiring from the outside. As you continue to grow, there may be specific positions where you want to hire someone from the outside, or you may not have a choice if there is no one currently serving in your ministry with the three Cs to fulfill the position that you have posted. However, for all the aforementioned reasons, and to show your volunteers that it is quite possible to one day get paid for what they are willing to do for free, hire from within whenever you can.

MAINTAIN A CULTURE OF FEEDBACK

My staff knows I have an open-door policy, and they can respectfully confer with me about anything. I value, love, and trust their judgment. I look forward to hearing their thoughts. They are open and honest because I often tell them (and show them) how important they are to me. I frequently challenge them to suggest new ideas and I implement them when appropriate. I give them the latitude to administrate their areas without micro-managing them. If you empower your leaders by allowing them to freely convey their concerns, you'll cultivate a culture of comfortable conversation, even when conflict is at the core of it. Your staff should feel at ease approaching you when they have an issue, idea, or need to discuss a sensitive matter. When they feel at liberty to share, it prevents subversive tendencies, wards off the spread of toxicity that unhappy employees instigate, and keeps you in tune with what the climate of your organization is.

Periodically throughout the year, we have staff professional days, where we do team-building exercises and have friendly contests where they assemble in teams and compete against one another for cash prizes. These types of collaborative activities build unity, boost morale, and bolsters confidence. As a result, even the most introverted staff members are more expressive. Allow your staff to share their views, even if it's a constructive critique of something you initiated. Doing this will encourage the mutual exchange of ideas and foster a healthy culture for you and your staff.

According to Dr. Chand, there are several characteristics of inspiring cultures. Here are just a few:

- The leaders of these organizations give clear direction, but they aren't authoritarian; they value the input of every person. Authority is decentralized.

- Leaders cultivate an atmosphere of trust and respect.

- There is a powerful synergy between relationships and organizational goals.

- The organization invests significantly and systematically in creating and building a healthy culture.[25]

STAFF YOUR WEAKNESSES

I hire people who are much smarter than me in their particular area of expertise. I just learned to type last year, and if I had to balance our checking account every month, my wife and I would be in trouble. I'm just not good at certain things; therefore, I have to hire people who complement my shortcomings. Surround yourself with humble people who know much more than you do. Not only will this lead to your church's growth, this will grow you as well. You'll learn from your staff. And after all, who needs two of you?

I'm a visionary and like most visionaries, I don't like details. I'm

25. Chand, Samuel, Cracking Your Church's Culture Code, (San Francisco: Jossey-Bass, 2011), 22.

always thinking ahead, and very seldom do I think about the logistics that it takes to accomplish many of the ideas I come up with. Not that I'm not aware that there are many moving parts necessary to carry out my vision; I'm very aware. But focusing on the details hinders my ability to focus on the big picture, so I need detailed people around me.

Chand describes people who are detail-oriented as managers, and visionaries need managers around them. He points out several distinctions between managers and visionaries. Here are some of them:

- Leaders take risks; managers avoid risks

- Leaders move quickly; managers move slowly

- Leaders are people centered; managers are system centered

- Leaders are idea centered; managers are plan centered[26]

Every dynamic, growing organization needs both leaders and managers. As the head, you need to be a leader, but frame your ministry with solid managers. Managers are a lot more rigid than leaders, but that's not a bad thing. You need some rigidity to maintain and build structure. Leaders are a lot more elastic than managers. You need some elasticity to create and reinforce structure.

---

26. Chand, Samuel, Cracking Your Church's Culture Code, (San Francisco: Jossey-Bass, 2011), 50.

/ FINANCE /

Every pastor that is serious about impacting his or her city is going to need some money. Relevant, 21st century ministry and money are inextricably linked. Everything costs money. Whether its evangelism, facilities, staffing, outreach, or pretty much anything else you can think of regarding ministry, it costs money. I constantly ask the young, up-and-coming pastors I mentor the same question, "How much money do you have in the bank?" I don't ask them to be nosy; I ask them because experience has taught me that finance is as important to the success of their ministry as any other area.

When a young ministry experiences exponential growth as we did in 2000, they also face a lot of what I call "good problems." I call them good problems because they are problems that the pastor down the street with no growth or momentum would love to have. Nonetheless, they are still issues that can impact your ministry. One such issue is finance.

The average pastor who has never experienced extraordinary growth looks from the outside and assumes your ministry is doing great financially because of all the people who are joining and visiting your young, exciting church. What they don't know is that because you are attracting people with no church experience or understanding of stewardship, they aren't trained givers yet. So even though the worship is awesome and people are getting saved by the tens each week, the offering sucks! People are only putting a dollar in church if anything at all. So yes, you had a thousand people in church, but your offering was only two or three thousand dollars, not the twenty thousand dollars onlookers assume.

Lack of giving creates one of the first major problems your wonderful, fast-growing church will experience. You have a lot of people with a lot of needs, but you have no money. Empathy from other pastors is virtually nonexistent because they assume that you are loaded and financially set for the rest of your life. Most times, the pastors of these fast-growing churches still cannot pay their mortgages on time, even after they have crossed the threshold into mega.

When he first starts a church, the senior pastor is making tremendous financial sacrifices to handle the massive overhead expenses that come with rapid growth. In their book *Beyond Megachurch Myths*, Scott Thumma and Dave Travis debunk many of the untruths, myths, and assumptions regarding megachurches and their leaders. One such myth is that most megachurch pastors are rich, live in big homes, and have one or more luxury cars. Regarding the issue of compensation, Thumma and Travis say this:

> *A question we often hear in any discussion of megachurch pastors concerns their compensation. The widely reported earnings of some big-name television preachers and the handful of pastors who derive significant income from book sales are far from the norm. Likewise, the press accounts listing details of expensive homes, multiple luxury automobiles, and other holdings are true for only a minority of pastors. While it is true that some megachurch*

pastors do have major income streams in addition to their salaries, in our experience these are rare exceptions to the norm.[27]

The reality is that most pastors experiencing accelerated growth are just trying to keep it all together financially, both from a personal and ministry perspective. I remember when we started "THE WORD" CHURCH, in one year we went from one hundred to seven hundred people attending weekly with no signs of letting up.

With that kind of growth we needed full-time staff to meet the overwhelming needs of a young, growing congregation. We needed office space because though the high school was great for our weekly services, there was no place to conduct spiritual guidance, have rehearsals, do leadership training, etc. (Notice I said spiritual guidance, not counseling. It is unwise to call it counseling until you have someone on staff who is degreed or at least certified in counseling. You leave yourself vulnerable to lawsuits if bad advice is given). All of the aforementioned activities require money for effective kingdom ministry.

Don't ever allow anyone to minimize the importance of finance in your ministry. A church with money can get stuff done. People today are struggling and need help spiritually and existentially. If you are going to touch people where they are hurting you are going to need the resources to do it.

THE AUTHORITY OF MONEY

While on sabbatical a few years ago, it dawned on me how much authority is connected to having money. Whether the link between having money and authority is right or wrong is beside the point. The fact is money gives you power. People or churches that are financially fit are afforded opportunities that others are not. When I returned

---

27. Thumma, Scott and Dave Travis, Beyond Megachurch Myths, (What We Can Learn from America's Largest Churches, (San Francisco: Jossey-Bass, 2007), 61.

from sabbatical, I taught a series titled "The Authority of Money" that challenged our people on the importance of financially positioning ourselves as a congregation in order to effectuate a positive change in the morale, conditions, and spirit of residents in the Greater Cleveland area—the area that God has assigned me to.

A couple of years ago, gas prices skyrocketed. People complained and could barely afford enough gas to get back and forth to work. I have learned over the years that it is in crisis that a church with resources can really show off for God. I decided to go on the secular radio stations in our city and announce that we were giving away $25,000 worth of gas at two local gas stations; $25 per car to anyone in need. No strings attached. The local media got wind of it and every news station in the area was there to cover it.

But it gets better. In order to maximize the event's impact, we decided that we would not announce the two gas stations until thirty minutes before the event and the announcement would be made over the radio. The local radio stations loved the idea because of the money they would make with listeners glued to their stations and supporting their sponsors, plus all the advertising we did, which made them money as well. The gas station owners loved it because what we spent with them nearly doubled the money they would have made on a Sunday afternoon when business is normally slower than usual.

Within minutes of announcing the locations of the two gas stations where the free gas would be given away, there were traffic jams extending for miles at both of them. People were literally running out of gas while waiting in the long lines and our men had to push their cars to the pump. Every local news station covered the event and some even had to use their helicopters because their news trucks could not get through the jam-packed traffic.

Though there are dozens of great stories and memorable

comments from that day, there is one lady I will never forget. She said to me, "Pastor Vernon, this is a great event but I was just thinking, couldn't you have just given out gas cards at your church so as to avoid all this traffic and craziness?" I looked at her and said, "Do you see those news helicopters in the air? Do you see all the hard-working police out here who we are paying for this event? Do you see how busy all the businesses on this street are this afternoon? Most of all, do you see all these people that are hugging my wife and me and seeing the love of Jesus Christ through what we are doing today? This is what I call 'kingdom chaos' and I love it!"

What she did not realize is that we wanted the attention. Yes indeed, every bit of the publicity we got, we wanted. For years, the question that churches (especially megachurches), have been asked is, "What do they do with the money?" Sometimes, you have to be intentional in letting the community see the church using its tithes and offerings to make a real difference in the community.

I will discuss the impact and biblical mandate of outreach in a later chapter, but the point is that the event captured our city's attention and would not have been possible without our church being in a strong financial position. Money allows you to have real impact in your city without grants, handouts, or other people's permission. Without finance, you become the average church getting together each week having a good time with no real impact.

Having resources gives our ministry the ability to touch thousands of lives in our area. Each weekday morning we are on television in the large part of the Northeastern Ohio region. Our broadcast airs in all the local prisons, detention centers, nursing homes and hospitals in our area. Whenever the local school systems have a pressing need that they cannot afford, they call on our ministry for everything from school supplies to sports uniforms and equipment.

People do not just need prayer; they need help with their utilities, food for their families, and all that goes with everyday survival in this arduous economy. No church can do it all, but without money you cannot do much of anything to help in these areas. Money even helps with evangelism.

I like to say it this way: the more money you have the more souls you can go after; the more souls you get saved and trained in giving, the more money your church will have to go after more souls. It might sound unspiritual and even carnal to some, but it is truth nonetheless. You need finance to do effective evangelism and kingdom ministry. If you want to send out a street team to witness they should at least have some tracks to pass out with the message of Jesus and your church's website. Guess what? Those tracks cost money. If you want to feed the hungry in your church's neighborhood, it costs money. If you want to do GED training or any other educational programs, again, you need finances.

WATCH YOUR DEBT

The most important advice I can give any pastor is to avoid debt. Most growing churches find themselves in a position where they need more space because they are quickly expanding and since their financials show a steady increase in revenue, some bank or lending institution will in most cases loan them the money they need to build or purchase a new or existing facility.

It has been my experience that it is best to do what you have to do to avoid borrowing money. Whether it is moving to multiple weekend services, renting another building or whatever, do not borrow money! Just wait until you can pay cash. Debt takes away some of the authority I have been talking about. When you owe, you do not own, the bank does. This then gives them the authority to demand your financial statements each year and to tell you how much money you must have on hand at all times in order to satisfy the covenants of the loan. If your finances drop beneath that agreed amount they can call your loan in full immediately and foreclose your building leaving your church scrambling for a place to worship.

There is a certain freedom that comes with owing no one anything. It allows you to move and shake for God without the pressure of a monthly note. Churches with good offerings and no debt can do more outreach, evangelism by television, radio ministry, pay their employees what they are worth, and do amazing stuff like pay cash for homes and automobiles for faithful members in need.

If the recent economic tsunami has taught us anything, it is that things can change financially in a second. Never in recent history have so many churches entered into foreclosure. Why? Because they built huge beautiful buildings with bank loans they could not pay when the recession occurred. Members stopped giving because they lost their jobs, which of course impacted their giving, but the banks said, "So what! We want our money or we're taking back our building."

Are there cases where using someone else's money makes sense? I don't believe so. By no means am I a financial expert on borrowing or any other area of money. As a matter-of-fact, I highly recommend Dave Ramsey's book, *The Total Money Makeover*, to pastors and churches seeking some great practical advice on debt and money in general.

GET SMART

Along with reading Ramsey's book on finance and increasing your business knowledge as the leader, as soon as possible, hire a financial genius. My CFO has an MBA in finance and is also an accountant. Most pastors invest in every area except the finance department.

For growing churches this is essential. For smaller churches that do not raise much money, a financial secretary who loves God is adequate.

When you are handling millions of dollars or you are quickly approaching those kinds of numbers, you need someone with financial training and a staff to help them. Yes, you will need an entire full-time finance department to ensure that your money is being handled effectively. At this level, with profit and nonprofit money coming in, with all the financial scrutiny that megachurch pastors are under you need competent financial people around you to keep everything separate and clean.

TEACH THEM HOW TO GIVE

As I said earlier, the reality is big membership does not necessarily equate to big offerings. People must be trained on the importance and biblical mandate of giving. They do not give by nature any more than they stop sleeping around, cursing, lying, gambling, cheating or anything else by nature. It takes the power of God's spirit coupled with bold Bible teaching to achieve these lofty but attainable goals. I believe that some pastors really do not know how, if, or when to teach on the subject of money. From conversations I have had with pastors around the nation, there seems to be a certain timidity birthed out of a fear of coming across as dishonest or deceptive.

If you're unsure of how to teach about money, feel free to get any of my messages on finance, which are available at our ministry website. My series called "The Authority of Money" is comprehensive; "Ten Reasons to Tithe," is another great teaching. Glean from them whatever you can and share it with your attendees.

There will always be critics; do not let them stop you from maximizing your church's financial potential. You must teach them how to give and why they should give. Be transparent about the church's finances. Explain to them the blessing of giving without promising them anything the Bible does not. Never beg. Just cast vision and they will respond. You'll see an increase in your offerings.

Remember this: PEOPLE DO NOT GIVE TO NEED, THEY GIVE TO VISION. If people gave to need, then the neediest organizations would have the most money. Everybody needs something, including your members. It is vision that ignites people to action. What caused people in Montgomery to walk miles to work in the rain in 1955 as opposed to catching a segregated bus? What caused 250,000 people to march on Washington on August 28, 1963? The answer to both questions is the vision of Dr. King. Vision both excites and challenges people to go above and beyond what they would normally do. To pastors who constantly fret and complain when offerings are low, is it possible that the vision and teaching on giving is low also?

TIMING IS EVERYTHING

Start a series on giving in January; everybody is willing to change in January. There is a freshness in the air. Over the years we have discovered that the first quarter of the year is our best giving quarter so we maximize it. Each year in January, I do a series on finance that involves tithing, giving, debt cancellation, the power of a church with unlimited resources, and how we can impact the city for God. If you do not start it in January, then September is another great month. People are coming back from summer vacations, kids are headed back to school and it is a good time to challenge people in the area of giving or even to begin a stewardship campaign before the holidays begin in November.

In most churches, the people who come to your midweek service are already giving; it is the weekend crowd that needs more pushing. Do not be afraid of the looks on their faces or think they are not enjoying it because they are quiet. The majority of them are struggling financially and are glad to be getting some clear Bible teaching on or about their money or the lack thereof.

PURE MOTIVES

I do not lose a minute of sleep over challenging our people to give because I know our church's assignment and how pure my motives are for wanting and needing money. We are called to feed the hungry and clothe the naked along with all the other things we do on a monthly basis that I will discuss in my chapter on outreach.

There are global missionaries who go into impoverished communities and bring messages of hope and inspiration to the people there. There are other pastors who are called to spread the Gospel of Jesus Christ across the nation. For them, they may need resources to pay for their travel expenses, or to pay for their mode of transportation. There is nothing wrong with having a jet if you need one to spread the Gospel of Jesus Christ and you have the resources to pay for one. At this level of ministry, the needs are different. For example, if a certain megachurch pastor has a church in New York and Atlanta, how do you propose he get back and forth between the two? Never allow people outside your ministry to dictate what you need.

I'm giving the city of Cleveland all I have and I make tremendous sacrifices. Because of who I am, my children are faced with certain inconveniences. I can't go to the local swimming pool and take my shirt off because women don't need to see me shirtless. It would be inappropriate for the men in my church to see my wife in a bathing suit. So, we have a home outside of Cleveland where we are slightly less recognizable, where my family and I can go to swim comfortably.

I decided a long time ago that if I was going to live in a bubble, it was going to be a big bubble. I find it interesting that people are offended when megachurch pastors leading 20,000 members have jets, but the pope can fly around on a private jet and no one says anything. I don't mean any disrespect toward Catholic believers, but I have wondered why, generally speaking, that double standard exists.

Our call is not abroad; we are the city's church. It is not just our members that depend on us, but there are thousands of Clevelanders who lean on our ministry in hard times. There is a certain amount of money required to perform the philanthropic tasks we tackle on a daily basis. We need a lot, God can trust us with a lot, and therefore He gives us a lot. For that I do not apologize.

Every pastor must ask themselves the question, "Why do I really want big offerings?" Do not feel bad if your first thought is financial security for your family. That does not make you a crook. That just means you are a husband and father who wants his family to be whole. However, if you do not have the heart of Jesus for hurting and needy people, I sincerely suggest you do something else to provide a living for yourself and your family.

To those of you who are called by God to do the kind of ministry described in Matthew 25:35-36, it will take finances to do it. The more money you have the better. Right now, with all the needs in the Cleveland area and my heart and vision to help lift it, how could our church possibly have too much money? Once you reconcile within your cognitive domain that your motives are pure, do not let any detractors prevent you from positioning both your family and ministry to be a blessing to the least and left out of our society. The only real way to help others is to have the necessary resources to help because poor people cannot help poor people.

TAKE CARE OF YOUR FAMILY

In their attempt to make sure the church is okay, many church leaders neglect their families. Many pastors, after 20 to 50 years of pastoring, have nothing to show for it. One of the things that many pastors do is juxtapose their lives with Christ, and believe that they should be poor because of the way Jesus lived when He was on earth. This juxtaposition is erroneous and causes pastors to abandon their familial assignments.

Jesus' assignment dictated His finance. My assignment is multifarious. I have six children that need college tuition paid for. My father-in-law was a pastor, and a great husband and father, but sadly, he died having never reached his monetary goals. He was so consumed with taking care of the church, that he didn't properly balance his other responsibilities. As a result, I take care of my mother-in-law now. His heart was in the right place, but because of a lack of education in financial planning and misappropriated goals, his widow had no financial security.

There are many pastors who leave their families in this very same situation, and there's no acceptable reason for it. I cannot stress it enough; look out for your family. When you become a megachurch pastor, theoretically, the list of people you become responsible for grows. Others will rely on you when they are faced with difficult circumstances because of their perception of what you have. Your family automatically makes the list; others you will need to permit a space on the list, but you should know that your extended family and close friends' expectations of you will increase. You'll need money to help meet those expectations.

Jesus wasn't married, and neither was Paul. They did not have many earthly assignments. If you don't plan to be married or own a home, follow Paul's model. To the other 99% of you who desire the love of the opposite sex, and will live past 33, make sure you plan for your family's wellbeing. There is no way I'm going to raise millions of dollars for years, and not have something for my family. I'm not going to feed everyone else and my own go hungry, or provide shelter for others, and not for my own. Anyone who knows me knows I have integrity.

MAINTAIN YOUR BALANCE

Preserve your mental and emotional margin by understanding your call and commitments. Because I have a national television broadcast, I am invited to speak at hundreds of events every year. However, this past year, I declined almost every invitation I received outside of those in or near the city of Cleveland.

Many pastors dream about traveling across the nation. In fact, it is a great part of the reason they even have a national broadcast—to have a presence on TV and to promote their personal ministry. There is nothing wrong with wanting exposure for your ministry if the motivation to be invited to speak is to get people saved and to improve the quality of the lives of those who are already saved. If the assignment on your life is to be an evangelist you should pursue it passionately.

The challenge with being an evangelist and a pastor is that both roles take a considerable amount of energy and devotion, and to do either effectively you have to put significant time in. Personally, I do not believe you can do everything well. Billy Graham is arguably the greatest evangelist that ever lived. Ever wonder why he didn't pastor a church? Certainly with a lifetime audience of over 2.2 billion people he could have established a church and had a plethora of faithful followers.[28] But perhaps, he recognized that his call was to evangelize, not to pastor, and chose to do the former.

---

28. "Billy Graham: A Man With A Mission Impossible, (Special Section)". Cincinnati Post. June 27, 2002.

If your goal is to be an effective pastor, better yet, an effective megachurch pastor, you cannot be an effective evangelist. If you only have a hundred members, you have a bit more liberty to travel abroad and minister in other cities on a regular basis. But a megachurch pastor, serious about building people and facilities, and concerned with establishing partnerships with community and city officials to bring programs and resources to their city and public school system cannot be gone two to three days a week. If I did nothing else other than staff meetings, touching key leaders, mentoring the pastors in my fellowship, and preparing for thirteen services a week, I would be doing more than enough.

If you are a gifted preacher, and have been exposed to preaching on a national or international level, the lure of evangelizing around the world can be great. Let's just be straight. Not only is there money in it, but the experience of traveling to different cities, learning different cultures, meeting other pastors and preachers, can be intoxicating. I'd also be remiss if I didn't mention one other temptation: the fascination of feeling like a celebrity.

When you preach at home, very few times do your members ask for your autograph or for you to take a picture with them. They see you every week, several times during the week in fact. As their spiritual father or mother, you're practically family. However, when you go to a city where the crowd has only seen you on TV, to them it feels like a rare opportunity to get close to someone they've only been able to admire from afar. I remember feeling surprised and overwhelmed at times by the amount of attention I was given after a speaking engagement. It was both humbling and invigorating to have people so touched that they are eager to share with me how my message motivated or inspired them.

I have to be honest. The feeling I just described is a great one. But for me, while my members don't regularly ask me for my autograph, they treat me exceptionally well. They affirm and encourage me consistently. Therefore, even when I did travel extensively, although it felt good to have others telling me how wonderful my sermon was, they weren't doing anything for me that I wasn't getting at home.

But, on the other hand, if I wasn't getting support at home, if my members were constantly bickering and complaining, and always criticizing my preaching, the pull to travel across the nation and receive all the complimentary (sometimes cursory) comments regarding my preaching would probably be a lot greater.

Check your motivation. Personal praise should not be your reason for being an evangelist. Eventually, that too will get old. Know your call and maintain your balance by being true to it and not stretching yourself across a spiritual spectrum. If you are called to be a megachurch pastor, chances are, you are not called to be a national evangelist.

I am not saying that you can't travel at all. Taking the truth of God's Word to the masses is important. What I am saying is that you cannot regularly travel across the globe and expect to grow your church at home.

As I write this, my wife and I are still relishing in the bliss of our newborn baby, and we have two other small children at home. Even though I am a megachurch pastor, I determined a long time ago that I would not neglect my children in the name of ministry. Outside of emergencies, I attend every game, recital, concert, and any other event that they're involved in. I keep my commitments to them. If I tell them we're going somewhere, we go. If I feel like my ministry schedule is imposing on their time, I make adjustments to it. I spend time with them, I talk to them, I play with them, I pour into them.

If you do it right, and by "it" I mean pastor and parent, your kids will not know just how mega you are. My children are able to lead "normal" lives because I make sure that I keep my commitments to them and I do not allow ministry to interfere with my fatherly duties.

Of course, I could not handle all that I do without a great support system, starting with my wife. Beyond her, I have surrounded myself with staff members who clearly understand what my life goals and priorities are, and they keep my ladder steady while I continue to climb. What I'm about to say next may sound simplistic, but I think the significance of this idea is important enough to run the risk of oversimplifying.

Surround yourself with people who recognize, respect, and value your personal and professional objectives. You can only go as high and as far as your foundation will permit. I don't have to tell you what happens when you try to build on a weak foundation. Your ladder holders don't necessarily have to share your objectives, so long as they are willing to effectually support them. This is especially true of your key staff members and inner circle, and is a non-negotiable. If they are incapable or unwilling to help you get to your desired destination by contributing to your life in meaningful, useful ways (and you have to determine what that looks like), then you must reevaluate those who you have elected to have in that area of your life and perhaps shift some people around.

KEEP YOUR FINANCES CLEAN

Megachurches attract a lot of scrutiny because of the amount of money they bring in, and get into legal trouble because they don't properly balance their books. Make sure you do internal audits and maintain your national and/or state guidelines for bookkeeping. As far as your salary, how much you make should be directly in line with how much you are taking in. If your church is in a good place financially, you should be too. If not, you should hold off on salary increases, luxury vacations, and expensive purchases until it is. If you are still endeavoring to get to at least a moderate level of growth and finance, do not make the mistake of taking too much before you've earned it. Be patient. I don't know if 200 members and a Bentley makes sense.

Having a megachurch magnifies every issue that smaller churches have. One of the few benefits once you get your ministry to a comfortable place is financial security. In this line of work, you have double the stress, sometimes resulting in a shorter lifespan. The only worry that we do not have is how we will pay our house note. When you work hard to get your church out of debt, teach, preach, lead souls to Christ, create programs, etc., there is no reason why you shouldn't benefit from your hard work, presumably, as you would in any other occupation. But, to make sure you're on track, have a financial advisor do a compensation analysis for you so that you know how much you should make and how much you should be putting away for your family.

STREAMS OF INCOME

It's very important as a pastor that your earning power and potential is diversified between a number of different ventures. All of my income is not from "THE WORD" CHURCH. You're reading one of two books I've written, and others are in the works. I have a record label and publishing company, and a real estate company. My outside ventures could handle my monthly bills if I never received another check from "THE WORD" CHURCH. With Cleveland and pastors on my mind, that's easier to do when I'm not worried about money myself.

Having multiple streams of income is wise, but the concept is also biblically applicable. Bishop T.D. Jakes did a wonderful teaching some years ago on the four streams in the Garden of Eden in Genesis 2, Pishon, Gihon, Tigris, and Euphrates, and metaphorically contextualized them to relate to sources of income. In the Garden there was one river, and it branched off into four different brooks. The division of the river into four brooks, or streams, could be symbolic of expanding your ability to earn a living between various enterprises.

SIZE DOES MATTER

CHAPTER SEVEN

/ OUTREACH /

There are two passages in the New Testament that helped to concretize our church's purpose and call. Jesus said in Matthew 25:35-36, "For I was hungry, and you gave me something to eat; I was thirsty, and you gave me something to drink; I was a stranger, and you invited me in; [36] naked, and you clothed me; I was sick, and you visited me; I was in prison, and you came to me."

In Luke 4:18, Christ gives His statement of purpose when He says: "The Spirit of the Lord is upon Me, because He anointed Me to preach the gospel to the poor. He has sent Me to proclaim release to the captives, and recovery of sight to the blind, to set free those who are oppressed."

These two Christological passages have become the foundation of our ministry. I have learned over the years that each church and pastor have their own assignment from God and that I should not be too quick to state emphatically what every church should be doing. However, I believe outreach is a call to the universal church that cannot be ignored.

SIZE DOES MATTER

When pastors ask me what they can do to gain momentum in their ministry, without hesitation my first answer is outreach. The church can no longer just embrace the soteriological Christ seen in John 3:16, but they must also engage the sociological Christ that is concerned with the existential plight of the poor found in the aforementioned Matthean and Lukan passages. Real Jesus ministry is helping the poor and those in need. It was Dr. King who said, "Any religion that professes to be concerned about the souls of men and is not concerned about the slums that damn them, the economic conditions that strangle them and the social conditions that cripple them is a spiritually moribund religion awaiting burial."[29] Every church, especially the Black Megachurch, should be constantly challenging itself in the area of outreach. We have the opportunity and the responsibility to make a difference in the lives of the hurting people of our neighborhoods.

I constantly challenge myself and our ministry with the same questions. Why did God cause us to become a megachurch in one of the poorest, frustrated, cities in America? To me, the answer is obvious. God needed a vessel to help lift our area—a church He could count on to take its resources and give back to the city it is situated in. The megachurch has an opportunity to shine in a dark world. Nothing is more satisfying for me as a pastor as when I go on television and radio to announce to the city that we are giving away free gas, free shoes to children, or bags of food to anyone feeling the effects of this arduous economy.

I recall reading a quote by Howard Thurman sometime ago that has remained with me ever since: "Ask not what the world needs. Ask what makes you come alive... then go do it. Because what the world needs is people who have come alive." Outreach causes our church to come alive! We have had the most popular speakers in the Christian

---

29. King, Martin Luther and James M. Washington (ed), I Have a Dream: Writings and Speeches that Changed the World, (Reading: Addison Wesley, 1986), 38.

community come to "THE WORD" CHURCH. We have had all sorts of major events, but nothing excites and drives our ministry like outreach.

OUTREACH AND CHURCH GROWTH

In the sixth chapter of John, Jesus has a crowd of people following Him and used the occasion to teach us a powerful principle concerning outreach and evangelism. Verse 5 says, "Therefore Jesus, lifting up His eyes and seeing that a large crowd was coming to Him, said to Philip, "Where are we to buy bread, so that these may eat?" The point was simple: you cannot preach to people until you address their everyday needs.

The disciples, like many churches today, were content with ignoring the needs of the masses because of what they perceive to be a lack of resources, but Jesus tells them to look in the crowd to see if there is anything to get started with. Every church can do something. Megachurches can and should do more because of their resources and people power, but every church can look in the crowd for something to get started with.

If you are a small church or a church without plenteous resources, I have a great inexpensive outreach event for you to try. Take a warm Saturday in the summer and host a free food and carwash event. Get a large, professional, sign that says, 'FREE CARWASH! FREE FOOD AND DRINKS WHILE YOU WAIT!' Little do they know that the free food and drinks are hotdogs and lemonade, but all you promised on the advertisement was free food and drinks. You never said what kind, did you?

Hopefully, your church is situated on a busy street. If not, get permission from a popular business in the area to use their parking lot. Most will not mind because your event will attract even more customers to them that day. The fact that your sign says 'FREE' is going to draw many people. As they pull in, make sure your people do an excellent job washing and shining the tires of each vehicle. Serve the hotdogs and drinks with kindness and professionalism. Do not preach to them while they wait for their vehicle to be completed; just let them enjoy their meal in peace. As they leave, have your most pleasant people give them a packet about your ministry and a loving smile. The entire event should cost no more than a couple hundred dollars, but the impact will be priceless.

How can this type of outreach event affect your church's growth? Consider this: If I am a sinner or an individual with no church home seeking a place to go on Christmas, Mother's Day, Easter, or the first Sunday of the year (the major days people consider going to church), I will probably think of that nice church that washed my car, fed me, and treated me so kindly on that beautiful summer day.

Let us say that day you washed one hundred cars and the average car had about three people in it. Out of those three hundred people you touched that day maybe a tenth of them consider visiting your church. Out of the thirty people who visit maybe ten join. I would say the event was worth it. Hundreds of people have visited our church simply because we gave their child a backpack for school or gave their family groceries during a rough period of their life. I could go on and on telling you stories of how outreach has directly influenced the growth of our ministry.

THE MEGACHURCH MANDATE

I feel the Black Megachurch and megachurches as a whole must do large-scale outreach—events that capture and captivate the entire city. I believe that the very reason God gave us this unusual growth is to do unprecedented outreach events that literally arrest the attention of the media and the antagonist of the Christian agenda.

This past summer, our ministry spent over $100,000 on Word-Mart, an event we started a few years back where we give away school supplies, clothing, shoes, and food to needy children in the Cleveland area. I hugged thousands of parents who told me that they had no other means of getting shoes for their family. The thing that touched me the most was the amount of black men who hugged me, looked me in my eyes, and said, "Thanks for helping my child."

The event caused a certain ambivalence within me. On the one hand, as a father it saddened me to imagine the loss of dignity many of the black men there probably experienced waiting in long lines for our church to do for his child what he no doubt would have loved to do himself. On the other hand, I was rejoicing that we had the desire, and even more than that, the resources to do it.

Our most recent Word-Mart event was held at Progressive Field (home of the Cleveland Indians). Team officials offered us the entire stadium at no cost. When asked by media representatives covering the event why we give away so much and how we are able to do it, it afforded me the opportunity to speak to the power of God through the megachurch and explain that having resources allows us to meet real needs in the community.

Every single day I wake up and ask myself what else "THE WORD" CHURCH can do to help greater Cleveland. Outreach is simply what we do. We have a basic philosophy that I would recommend to all churches, especially growing churches or megachurches with significant resources. We pay the staff and bills each week, put something up for the future, and we give the rest away. We are not a for-profit business; we are a church. The tithes and offerings that the parishioners bring each week should be used to help hurting people. Though we have a couple of for-profit ventures, the objective of our ministry is outreach. We give away as much as we can.

Even our concerts and events are free. Recently, I invited Kirk Franklin, who is arguably the most sought-after Gospel music artist of our time, and told him I wanted to help lift the morale of our area with a citywide free concert. In order to accommodate what I knew would be close to 10,000 people, I called the mayor about using the Convention Center in downtown Cleveland.

While the event was free to the thousands that came, between paying Kirk, marketing on radio and TV, the use of the Convention Center, and all the media equipment necessary to make a concert viewable to a crowd that large, it ended up costing us nearly six figures for one night. Some might ask, "Why do that?" My short answer would be, "A megachurch has to do mega stuff!" There are people in our city that could never afford to go to a nice concert and see an artist of Kirk Franklin's caliber in person. It's our job to make certain morale-lifting luxuries are a reality in the life of poor people.

LISTED BELOW IS THE INVESTMENT IN OUTREACH BY

"THE WORD" CHURCH IN 2010:

OUTREACH ACTIVITIES FOR 2010
WORD South Food Pantry Averages
Number of Households Provided Food Each Month - 1,450
Total Number of People Provided Food Each Month - 2,040
Total Number of Households for Year - 17,400
Number Of People for Year - 24,480
Pounds of Food Distributed for Year - 165,894

- -

FARMER'S MARKET (APRIL - NOVEMBER)
Pounds of Fruits/Vegetables/Bread Distributed - 96,000

EAST CLEVELAND MOBILE FOOD PANTRY (October - December)
Number of Households Provided Food Each Month - 213
Total Number of People Provided Food Each Month - 395
Total Number of Households - 639
Total Number of People - 1,185

IN-REACH WEEKEND
Total Number of Bags of Food for All Locations Each Month - 1,350
Total Number of Bags of School Supplies for All Locations - 1,800
Total Number of Gas Cards Provided per Month - 200
Annual Investment - $24,000

GETTING "THE WORD" OUT LOCAL BROADCAST
Annual Investment - $165,724

MEAL FEEDINGS
Friendly Inn - Total Number of People Fed for the Year - 1,836
Teen Challenge - Total Number of People Fed for the Year - 564
Teen Challenge Grocery Delivery for the Year - $12,600

WORD MART (DOWNTOWN CLEVELAND, AKRON, WARRENS-VILLE, HOPE ACADEMY)
Total Number of Pairs of Tennis Shoes - 5,000
Total Number of Bikes for Students - 320
Total Investment - $100,995

$50 FRIENDS (APRIL - DECEMBER)
209 Recipients - $10,450.00

PAY-IT-FORWARD

Annual Investment - $57,175.00

MEN'S MONDAY GED TRAINING

Annual Investment - $14,880

MEN'S MONDAY FEEDING

Annual Investment - $7,200

SEMINARY TRAINING

Ministers in Training

Investment Total - $15,800

BENEVOLENCE

78 Families Served

Annual Cost - $38,000

GUEST PERFORMANCES/SPEAKERS

Annual Cost - $110,000

IN-REACH WEEKEND

We discovered some years ago that we were so busy touching the needs of those outside our church, that we had unknowingly neglected some of our own members. The assumption was that since they were receiving my teachings each week and trusting God with their tithes and offering, their needs were met. We found out that many of our most faithful ministry workers and givers were being affected by the enervating economy.

One of my staff members coined the term 'in-reach'. We decided that one weekend a month would be In-Reach Weekend. This would be the one weekend that we would not reach out to the entire Cleveland community, but rather we would reach inward to our members with free groceries, gas cards, gift cards, etc.

After each service at all of our locations, during In-Reach Weekend we have U-Haul trucks full of bags of food for every member in need. Not just any kind of food, but food that I would take home to my family. I made it clear that I want our people to be given the best food and necessities we can afford each month. In addition, we have purchased four cars for members in need and gave a fully furnished home to a faithful couple in our church with four small children.

Our people respect and appreciate us blessing them each month and they reciprocate their gratefulness with their tremendous weekly giving, which helps us to keep giving. Jesus said in Luke 6:38, "Give, and it will be given to you. They will pour into your lap a good measure—pressed down, shaken together, and running over. For by your standard of measure it will be measured to you in return." This scripture has manifested many times over in the life of "THE WORD" CHURCH.

Every pastor, whether you pastor a large or small church, should commit to some level of outreach. Not only does outreach reflect Jesus' heart and goals in both the Matthew 25:35-36 and Luke 4:18 passages that I believe all churches should model, but it gives your members a sense of purpose and community.

Unequivocally, we have more people volunteer for outreach events than anything else we undertake. The members love the idea of coming together and making a difference in the community, and quite frankly, I favor our church participating in activities of this sort as opposed to insulating ourselves from the real needs of people and substantiating myths about megachurches not caring about the poor.

SIZE DOES MATTER

CHAPTER EIGHT

/ MARKETING /

So many churches are stunting their growth because of some sort of thwarted allegiance to traditional methodology. They refuse to embrace the modern times in which we live, where in order to attract certain people, churches must be intentional in the area of marketing and branding their ministries. There are over four hundred thousand churches in America, seemingly one on every other corner. The question I ask pastors across the nation who attend our training is, "Why should I come to your church? What would make the average person seeking a church home pick you guys? Are you depending on the sovereignty of God to show people where your church is and what you have to offer?"

There is nothing sinful or carnal about marketing and branding your ministry. As a matter-of-fact, it is biblical. In Luke 14, when teaching the parable of the dinner, Jesus said in verse 23, "And the master said to the slave, 'Go out into the highways and along the hedges, and compel them to come in, so that my house may be filled.'" The word 'compel' in the text suggests persuading people to come. The job of the church is not to sit back apathetically and wait for our ministries to grow, but rather to do all we can in the natural to facilitate that growth.

One of the greatest misconceptions among truly sincere pastors is that their commitment to Christ and their families will automatically lead to their ministries growing. In most cases that is simply not the reality. Rick Warren says:

> I know hundreds of dedicated pastors whose churches are not growing. They are faithful to God's Word, they pray earnestly and consistently, they preach solid messages, and their dedication is unquestioned—but still their churches refuse to grow. It is an insult to say that their problem is a lack of dedication. Few things infuriate me faster. These are good, godly pastors who serve God wholeheartedly. It takes more than dedication to lead a church to grow; it takes skill.[30]

One such skill Warren is referring to is the skill of marketing. You do not have to have a degree in marketing to do it effectively, but you do need the natural skill or someone to show you how to do it effectively. In this chapter, I will give you some step-by-step methods of branding and marketing, which without question has caused thousands to visit and in many cases join our ministry. Out of the over 400,000 churches in America, there are only about 1,400 megachurches.[31]

Every church is not going to be a megachurch or even a very large church, but I would argue that most churches could possibly be bigger if they really worked at it and considered implementing some marketing strategies. There are also very large churches at the precipice of becoming mega that either reject or lack the drive to go to the next

---

30. Warren, Rick, The Purpose-Driven Church, (Grand Rapids: Zondervan, 1995), 56-57.
31. Thumma, Scott and Dave Travis, Beyond Megachurch Myths: What We Can Learn from America's Largest Churches, (San Francisco: Jossey-Bass, 2005), 6.

level by marketing their already successful ministries.

In his book, *The Very Large Church*, Lyle E. Schaller writes:

> *Why have so many congregations plateaued in size with an average worship attendance in the 500 to 700 range rather than continuing to grow? One part of the explanation is that the leaders were content to perpetuate the congregational culture that is appropriate for a large church rather than revise it to a set of assumptions, values, and expectations appropriate for a megachurch.[32]*

BRANDING

Most megachurches have done a good job of branding themselves. In his book *Aqua Church*, Leonard Sweet discusses how the most successful companies in the world can at least in part attribute that success to thoughtful branding:

> *In many ways, the process of "branding" your church is the postmodern equivalent of "planning processes" (short term, long term, strategic) so beloved by moderns. Unlike mainline denominations, companies now offer what are being called "brand experiences" through "brand franchises" and "brand identities" so that you can feel a sense of community with others just through phrases like "Just Do it" (Nike) or "Think Different" (Apple). What does your church stand for? How will your church communicate its message to a postmodern culture? These are questions postmodern church leaders must ask and answer.[33]*

Every church needs a logo, something that identifies your church without your name on it. When people see the logo, they think about

32. Schaller, Lyle E., The Very Large Church, (Nashville: Abingdon Press, 2000), 22-23.
33. Sweet, Leonard I., AquaChurch 2.0: Piloting Your Church in Today's Fluid Culture, (Colorado Springs: Group Publishing, 2008), 176-177.

your church. Nike has the checkmark; McDonald's has the golden arches. What does your ministry have that makes it unique? Every church should hire a company that specializes in branding as soon as possible. A good branding company will meet with you, hear your vision as to what your church stands for, and then create a logo that reflects that.

WHAT IS YOUR MOTTO?

Every church also needs a short sentence or two that speaks to who you are. Not a sermon, just something short and catchy that will stick in people's mind when they read it. At "THE WORD" CHURCH our motto is simply "Come as you are, you won't stay as you are." Because our primary target is people with no prior church experience between the ages of 18 and 45, we realize many of the people we attract have a tattered past they are not proud of and many of them are still drinking, selling or using drugs, partying, having sex out of wedlock, and everything in between.

I cannot tell you how many people have said to me, "Pastor Vernon, I don't want to come to church until I get myself together." Of course my response to them is, "If you could get yourself together, you would be together already. Just come as you are." So with that in mind we came up with that motto when we started and it still holds true today.

STRATEGIES FOR MARKETING

One of my few natural talents is marketing. I have several people in our ministry who majored in marketing who are blown away with our church's ability in the area of marketing. To those pastors who want to do all you can in the natural realm to promote growth in your ministry, following are some marketing strategies that have proved invaluable at "THE WORD" CHURCH over the last decade or so. I intentionally listed them beginning with the least expensive strategies in order to be sensitive to pastors with an infinitesimal amount allotted for marketing in your yearly budget.

SEVEN WAYS TO MARKET YOUR MINISTRY

1. YOU'RE INVITED CARDS

Most churches invest in flyers with their church's information printed on them, however, they are normally too large to fit in the pockets or wallets of the members. The average person ends up setting them down somewhere, which defeats the purpose. Print wallet-size cards with your church's information (the website if you have one, address, phone number, church motto if it can fit legibly, and weekend service times).

Even if you are currently having one Sunday service, use the term 'Weekend Service' because it suggests growth in the future. Have directions to your church on the back of the card. Personally, I do not recommend putting your picture on the card. It takes up space and how you look is really irrelevant, and in some cases maybe even a deterrent. One Sunday a month, give each member at least four cards to put in their wallet. Instruct them to pass them out to four people they know, or random strangers they meet by chance. To this day with thousands of people in attendance, we still give each member four "You're Invited" cards one weekend a month.

2. SOCIAL MEDIA

Whether its Facebook, Twitter, YouTube, or e-blasts, take advantage of every social media outlet available. Like it or not, it is the 21st century means of communication for the world. Do not be the last church in America without a website. A website is quite possibly more important than a phone number to potential visitors. Hire someone or use a volunteer in your church to head up the social media ministry. If you do not, you will find that your church will quickly become archaic in the area of technology.

3. LICENSE PLATE COVERS

Connect with a company in your city that makes license plate covers, have them put your church's name at the top and your website at the bottom (There is not room for much more). Give a free cover to every member of your church when they join. This is great marketing for your ministry! Whenever someone pulls behind any of your members at a red light or stop sign, or if they are stuck in slow traffic, they will see the name of your church and website. God may use that license plate cover to get them to visit. You never know who is searching for a church but have no idea where to start.

We have learned over the years that it is best to have your parking people or any volunteer to drill them on the members' cars for them. People have a tendency to put them down and never get around to putting them on, which is a waste of your church's resources. Thousands of cars in Greater Cleveland have our church's name on their license plates. Even members who do not come anymore or have changed churches in most cases never remove it. We do not mind at all. It's free marketing!

4. CLOTHING AND OTHER APPAREL

A member with your church's name on their clothes, hat, coat, etc., is a walking billboard for your ministry. We keep our bookstore full of stuff with our name and website on it. When members have on clothing with their church's name and logo on the front and back, they are effortlessly marketing that ministry. Whenever you have a big event coming up, create a t-shirt or sweatshirt for it depending on what season of the year it is. This creates energy, church spirit, and of course, it serves as a marketing tool for your ministry. Never put the date of the event on the shirt; this way your people can continue wearing it when the event is over.

5. BILLBOARDS

Billboards are a great marketing tool. Drivers look up at billboards as they pass them on the street or highway. Why not let them see your church's name and website on one of them? Get as many as you can afford. Always make sure the light on the billboard is working. If it is not functioning properly people cannot see it at night and you forfeit half the marketing time you have paid for.

Also, ride by each board personally before you pay for it to make sure you can see it easily from your car. Remember, if you cannot see it, neither can anyone else.

Lastly, avoid being wordy in your ad. Less is more when it comes to billboards. People are driving or riding and only have a couple seconds to read it. A professionally photographed picture with your name if you choose, your church's name, your website, and your motto are probably sufficient. If it gets too cluttered with information, people won't remember any of it. Another great place to put your church's info is on the back of the local buses in your city. They serve as riding billboards that expose your ministry to an amalgam of people.

6. RADIO

The Christian community needs to infiltrate the airways with the good news of Jesus as much as possible, which means that you should utilize both Christian and secular radio stations for marketing. At "THE WORD" CHURCH, we seldom market anything on Christian radio because most people who listen already have a church. Our target is the unsaved and with our target in mind we put our money where our audience is listening, the Hip-Hop and R & B stations. I was told by the presidents of the secular stations in our area that we were the first church that ever crossed over to their market. It costs significantly more to advertise on secular stations than religious stations, but for us the investment and the return are well worth it.

7. TELEVISION

Television is the most expensive and far-reaching of all the marketing methods. If your commercial plays during primetime or during the news hour, you could very well be seen by a half million people at one time. You cannot beat that. Because of the cost, this medium of advertising is primarily for very large churches or megachurches looking to take over for Jesus. If you can afford it, I say go for it!

About a year ago, we partnered with the most popular local news station in our area on something called "Pay it Forward." Viewers write in via the news station website and recommend a munificent person who could use some extra money themselves. The news station anchor then goes to that person's home or job and presents them with $400. Our ministry gives the news station over $1,000 a week to sponsor Pay it Forward. Consequently, when the anchor shows up with the live cameras rolling, they say in front of hundreds of thousands of viewers, "On behalf of the members of "THE WORD" CHURCH, we would like to present you with $400." Following the segment, they give me 15 seconds to say whatever I like to the entire news audience. It airs three times a week on the hottest news station in Cleveland. We spend close to $60,000 a year for it, but it has given us mainstream appeal that we never would have had.

Every church and pastor should make a commitment to market your ministry on some level. Word of mouth has proven over the years to be our most effective tool of evangelism. When people are excited about their church, they invite people. Never abandon one-on-one evangelism or personally inviting people like the woman at the well who told people to "Come see a man..." At the same time, consider these seven marketing tools and see if one or more of them makes sense from both a financial and strategic perspective.

THE POWER OF A GOOD NAME

When starting a church, choosing the right name is critical. The name should be short and easy to remember. The rule of thumb for a name is the shorter the better. Why should your name have any more than four words? Use a name that does not presuppose one's spirituality. Why call yourself the "Prophetic, Pentecostal, Episcopalian, Apostolic Church Incorporated?" If Pookie and Ray-Ray walk past your church, why would they want to come in? They don't even understand what your name means. Your name should be welcoming to non-believers. Christians already have a church, and "He is who is well does not need a physician." Appeal to the lost. Inevitably, every well-liked church is going to attract people from other ministries; however, those are not your target. You should only use a spiritual name if your goal is to attract believers.

Call me a proud father because I feel I have the best name in the country. I nicknamed the first church I pastored "THE WORD" CHURCH, and the leaders of the church would question me about it. Looking back now, I was pregnant with my current ministry but I didn't know it. Because that name was already in my spirit, it was a no-brainer for me to use it when I actually did start my own ministry. It captured who we were and what we were about in simplified terms.

Also, be careful with the word 'international' unless you know that God is calling you overseas. We are the city's church, so I didn't add international. Though it may prove difficult, keep it to three or four easy-to-understand words. One of the pastors I cover spiritually named his church "THE ROCK" Church. It's simple and catchy.

DENOMINATIONS

Some of the greatest megachurches in the nation are connected to denominations. But denominations define you. If you belong to a denomination, I'm not advising you to leave, but when you post your denominational designation on your sign, you label yourself. There are certain people who will not walk into a church that has a denominational classification on the end. Though your church may be free from traditional rules, people assume that they'll have the same experience that they've had at other churches of the same name. Think about it. Wherever you travel, you expect all McDonald's to have the same taste. You would be disappointed if they said, "We cook our Big Mac's differently than the other McDonald's."

For me, denominational titles are too limiting and I don't want sinners or seekers to define me by the restrictions of them. You can't say, "I'm of the C.O.G.I.C. faith, but we don't flow like traditional members of the C.O.G.I.C. denomination." Have you ever considered that in some ways it is disrespectful to your denomination to keep their name but have your own flow? If you have a denominational name, you should keep with the traditions of that denomination or ask yourself, "Should I leave my denomination? Does the flow of the denomination align with what God has given me?" If you answer these questions honestly, you'll be able to make a decision on what you need to do.

If God is calling you away from your denomination, then have the courage to drop the name. I got my rearing in the Baptist church from preachers like Caesar Clark and C.L. Franklin; Emmanuel Scott and Jasper Williams. Each year when I attended the National Baptist Convention, I would sit in the pastors' sessions and hone my craft of preaching based on what I learned and observed.

After being locked out, I realized that my denomination was too restrictive. Out of respect for the denomination, I left it. It worked for them but not for me. I'm out of the box. I don't know what God is going to do and I can't be limited by the restrictive norms of a particular denomination. To that end, being an independent megachurch works for me. If it's not attenuating your attendance, keep the denominational name.

My recommendation to those of you who are starting a ministry is to keep the name simple and to the point. The one benefit of having a denominational title is that people know what you believe when they look at your name. Thus, when you don't have a denominational disclaimer, it is important to define exactly what you believe. You have to be intentional and purposeful in delineating your doctrine. People need to know what you believe and what your pneumatological position is (what you believe about the Holy Spirit).

People should also know the tenets of your stance on Christology. Those of the protestant faith believe certain things; those of the apostolic faith believe certain things. Religions are birthed out of differing views of God. Differences in pneumatology, and soteriology, the study of salvation, all contribute to conflicting spiritual views and the formation of religious factions. For example, are you a cessationist based on your interpretation of I Corinthians 13, "where there are tongues they will cease?" The charismatic position, and the one that I ascribe to is that the gifts of the Spirit are very much alive--that separates us.

At "THE WORD" CHURCH, because of my Baptist rearing, I believe Jesus Christ is Lord and that professing Him as Savior is the only prerequisite to be saved. Unlike Baptists, I believe in all the gifts of the spirit. My pneumatological beliefs are closer to the charismatic community, while my soteriological beliefs are closer to the evangelicals. Consequently, this is one of the reasons why I don't fit with any group in our city. Most of the evangelicals think I've lost my mind and the charismatics don't think I'm saved.

When you don't fit into any group, you find yourself on an island. People like things with labels. Who would walk into a grocery store and buy something with no label? At "THE WORD" CHURCH we are charismatic, but not too much so. The downside for people who join our ministry is, there is no way to succinctly describe everything we believe, so you must sit through our new members classes to get a comprehensive understanding. If you are a young, up and coming ministry, I would advise you not to limit yourself to any particular denomination. But do what works for you. The main point is to distinguish and define your ministry as clearly as possible.

CHAPTER NINE

/ CREATIVITY /

About five years ago, I was watching television and I noticed something that had never been so obvious to me. I looked and sounded like all of my contemporaries. There were some slight differences, but for the most part we all had the same preaching flow, dressing style, stage look, etc.

At that moment I made a conscious decision that would catapult our ministry to the next level of greatness for God. I decided that I would no longer imitate or copy anyone and that I would do whatever it took to discover my own voice and call in ministry.

What was strikingly odd about my decision to resist conventional preaching styles is I later discovered that to everyone else, I was already a rebel. I had left my denomination and started a church in a school, which, at that time, was a radical move for Cleveland. My friends in my former denomination thought I was wrong for leaving and so they abandoned me. The Pentecostal pastors did not accept me because they thought I was still a cessationist. I fully believed and accepted the gifts of the Spirit. My soteriological position was and still is more in line with my former Baptist denomination than theirs.

As a result, I found myself alone at 30 years old, seeking significance and acceptance. Our church was exploding and with no one in my city to turn to, I formed friendships across the nation. Several of my friends in other cities were experiencing the same sort of growth as I was. Most of us were in our early 30s preaching on national television and taking the world by storm. The problem for me was that in a sense, I was still dealing with an identity crisis. Who was I? What was my church's purpose? What was our style and culture?

On the one hand I was preaching "come as you are," but on the other hand I was wearing a $1,000 suit, $500 shoes, and a $100 shirt each weekend. By no means is there anything wrong with dressing up, but it was antithetical to the culture I was trying to create. I felt God was doing something else, but my traditional rearing, coupled with my friends on television, was slowly killing the creativity God was calling me to.

That day as I was sitting there watching TV, I decided to change everything. From that day till now we have been an out-of-the-box, radical church that has impacted hundreds of pastors and churches across the nation with our creative culture. I pray that this chapter will assist you in discovering your church's uniqueness.

WHY CREATIVITY?

In his book *The Creative Leader*, Ed Young tells the story of a friend he went to college with. The young man was handsome, athletic, and just an all-around great guy. Ed had been witnessing to him and slowly trying to win him to Christ. Finally, one night the young man accepted Christ in Ed's dorm room and the next step was to get him involved in a local church. Young tells the story this way:

After Scott bowed his knee to Christ, I invited him to the church

I was attending, and for the first time, I began to see the church through someone else's eyes. The terminology was confusing. The music was tired. The overall feeling was lifeless and just plain boring. If I ever go into church work, I thought, I will do whatever it takes to provide a biblically driven, compelling, and creative experience that someone like my friend Scott could understand. I wish I could tell you that Scott is doing well, but the last time I heard from him, he was still floundering.[34]

Most people I encounter have nothing against God. They just do not like church! Somehow, we have allowed our worship experiences and preaching to become predictable. As much as I loved and will always love my home church, it was exactly the same every Sunday, so much so until I still remember the order of service over a decade removed. I think every pastor should at least consider some creativity in your service. Shake it up a little; do not let them figure you out. Dare to be different.

From a biblical perspective, the first thing every creative pastor must reconcile is that there is no biblical model on how to conduct your weekend services. It is just not there. From Acts through the Epistles we see nothing that tells us the order of service or when and if the choir should sing. The point is that every pastor has the liberty to create a culture that breeds and invites creativity both in your worship and in ministry as a whole.

CREATIVE CLOTHES

For me it began with how we dressed. I grew up in a culture that suggested you wear a suit and tie to church every Sunday. Let me say right away that there is absolutely nothing wrong with a suit and tie. The President wears one in about 95% of his public appearances. Dr.

---

34. Young, Ed, The Creative Leader: Unleashing the Power of Your Creative Potential, (Nashville, Tennessee: B&H Publishing Group, 2006), 10.

King always wore a suit and tie. But whom are you trying to attract and what culture are you trying to create?

My target was young people from urban areas between the ages of 18 and 35 at that time, so suits every Sunday did not fit for us. The first thing I did was gathered my staff and key leaders and shared my heart with them. I had to inculcate the vision of creativity and radical change into my team first so they could help me lead our church there. I shared with them that starting the following weekend, we would dress casual; suit and ties were no longer required. As a matter-of-fact, for the first few months we would be intentional in our casual dress in order to help shift the atmosphere.

Right away, a certain liberation came over our ministry and we saw an immediate positive impact on our attendance. Though I had never demanded that our men wear suits, people tend to dress how the leader dresses. Because I wore a suit, the men of our church wanted to dress like me. The problem was that many of them could not afford to dress that way each week. Our dress-how-you-feel policy has become a staple at "THE WORD." The only thing we ask is that our women not wear tight or seductive clothing. By nature, men are aroused by sight and so my wife and I really challenge our women leaders especially to wear loose, appropriate clothing. We ask our people not to wear anything with wording or pictures that are inappropriate for church. Other than that you can pretty much wear what you like.

In my chapter on preaching style I discussed how I dress—season-appropriate and befitting to the series I am preaching. I dress creatively according to what I am preaching and it works for me. Very seldom do I wear a tie during our weekend services; it is just not who we are. For some pastors reading this whose churches are not growing and you are searching for something to shift the momentum, how about starting with an eight to ten week experiment? Suggest to your congregation that everyone dress down the next couple of months. Summer is a great time to try this. Also, use this time to really push evangelism and invite people to dress down when they visit. If you and your people love it and it produces growth, stick with it. If not, you can always go back in the fall.

CREATIVE STAGING

Another major shift for me was changing the look of our stage. Notice I did not call it my pulpit. I do not view it as sacred; I see it as the place where I stand so everyone can see me. Most churches have what I call 'king's chairs,' including a seat for the pastor, which is normally slightly taller than the other ones. First of all, I am not the King, Jesus is. Secondly, it fits the traditional model that I am personally trying to avoid. I sit on the floor with the rest of the congregation.

As it relates to our weekend and weekday services, I try not to do anything precisely the same way all the time so as to avoid rigidity and legalism. My advice to you is to leave your stage area empty so you can be creative. I do not even have a choir stand. My choir sings on risers and then they come down.

Do not have anything permanent on the platform. Permanent fixtures confine you. Bear in mind my choice of words. I did not say "my" platform; I said "the" platform. Our stage is meant to glorify God, not me. During praise and worship, our singers, band, and dancers use it. We have an active arts ministry. On any given weekend, someone is up there rapping, miming, acting, or artistically expressing themselves in some way. My philosophy is that when they are on the stage, it is theirs for that moment because God is using them to edify and bless our people. When it is my time, I go up and do my part. And yes, women can go up there without God being angry. Welcome to the 21st century.

CREATIVE PODIUM

Most pastors have a stationary wooden or glass podium that for the most part never moves from the center of the stage. There is nothing biblical about the podium; that is just what most of us saw growing up and when we became pastors we got a podium too— it is just that simple. Because I do not believe it is my stage, I also do not believe the podium I use during my message should obstruct the congregation's view of the praise team and everyone else who ministers before I get up.

Instead of the traditional, stationary podium, we decided to design a podium with wheels on it. This way, we are able to roll it out when it is time for me to speak and roll it away when I am done. Another thing I like about having a rolling podium is that it allows me to work the stage without leaving my notes. I am not a manuscript preacher but the seminarian in me believes in writing my sermon each week and taking it up there with me even if I do not use all of it.

Because we have such a large sanctuary and stage, I try to work the room by walking from side to side as opposed to never leaving the podium, unlike pretty much all of the preachers I grew up watching and imitating. One of the reasons most pastors (especially manuscript speakers) never left the podium is because that is where the notes were. Having wheels on my podium allows me to move around and take my podium with me.

When we first designed the podium I was not trying to be a trendsetter. It just made sense for me. Little did I know at the time that hundreds of pastors who watch me on television across the nation would flood us with requests as to how they could get my rolling podium for their ministries.

CREATIVE PREACHING

The worst audience to preach to is one that has fallen asleep. Preaching does not and should not be boring and predictable. One reason among many that churches are not growing and sadly even declining is because the pastor's style of preaching is antiquated and lacks excitement. I am aware of many traditional pastors who would argue that style is irrelevant and that it is substance that matters, but I absolutely disagree. It does not matter how well prepared you are if no one is listening or paying attention.

Today's pastors must accept the fact that you are competing with so much more than pastors of the past. In the fast-moving, social media and technology-driven times in which we live people bore quickly. You must be willing to try new and innovative ways of getting your message across. Do not let them figure you out! Ed Young says regarding the traditional delivery of most pastors:

> Let me also suggest that you use a variety of approaches in your introductions. I know how easy and safe it is to come out week after week and use the same format for your messages. You tell a funny story, introduce the big idea, transition to your three main points and conclude with a summary and restatement of the big idea. That's not a bad approach, but it's also very predictable. If you're going to keep your audience guessing, if you're going to keep the connectivity high, you must keep the predictability low.[35]

I would give almost anything to convince pastors that you do not have to preach the same way each week. Some weekends, I use props in my message. Two of our most popular series of all times were on relationships. One was titled "Love, Sex, and Relationships," the other

---

35. Young, Ed, The Creative Leader: Unleashing the Power of Your Creative Potential, (Nashville, Tennessee: B&H Publishing Group, 2006), 114.

was called "I Can't Get No Satisfaction." In both series, I decided to preach from a bed that we placed right in the center of the stage. (You can do that when you do not have the king's chairs on the stage). Since the series was on relationships, my wife helped me teach several of the messages on marriage. When word got out that we were preaching from a bed, our attendance soared at all of our locations to the point of needing to use our overflow areas.

Might I suggest to critics of creative preaching that Jesus was creative and used illustrations all the time. In Matthew 6:26, He said, "Look at the birds of the air, they do not sow, nor reap, nor gather into barns, and yet your heavenly Father feeds them. Are you not worth much more than they?" I would argue that when He said, "Look at the birds…" it was because that was the perfect illustration for His crowd.

My educational mentor, Dr. Myers, said something during one of our doctoral courses that put into words what God had already revealed to me in my heart. He said that there are two realities that will and should impact your preaching and your worldview: the time in which you were born and your social condition. The fact that I was born in 1971 means that I am a part of the first generation of black pastors that grew up in the Hip-Hop generation. Not the blues, not Motown, but rap and R & B. Since most pastors attract a crowd that is around their age give or take a few years, most of my audience is between 30 and 45 and have similar issues and struggles, so I preach in a way that Generation X can relate to and enjoy. Each pastor must be willing to meet the crowd he preaches to where they are.

Creativity does not rob you of sound theological preaching. If anything, it enhances it. The message is the same, but the method should be ever-evolving with the changing times in which we exist. Several prominent pastors across the nation were invited by The Word Network to discuss the state of the Black Church. When challenged by one of the senior bishops on the panel as to why we young pastors refuse to adhere to what he viewed as the proven methodology of the days of old, Dr. Jamal Bryant, who pastors Empowerment Temple, a megachurch in Baltimore, Maryland, responded, "We're not trying to recreate the wheel, we just put some rims and spinners on it!"

CREATIVE TEAM

One of many great ideas I gained from reading Young's book was the need for a creative team. He said:

> No matter how creative you are, you will run out of steam and ideas fast if you try to do everything yourself. I've studied other communicators and discovered that the truly effective speakers have longevity in their ministries. One of the best ways to ensure longevity is by enlisting a creative team to help shoulder the joys and trials of ministry. You might say, "That's not for me. I am the man or I'm the woman; I can do it by myself. I'm strong enough. I'm autonomous enough. I'm big enough. I'm bad enough. I can create by myself." Sure you might be able to do it for awhile, but I'll tell you straight up that someday you will hit the wall.[36]

Look for the most creative people on your staff and invite them to become a part of your creative team. Keep in mind that everyone is not creative. Some people on your staff are great at what you pay them for but they do not necessarily think creatively. Draft people who are gifted to help you come up with creative illustrations and ideas to help improve and bring excitement to your sermon series and your ministry as a whole. My creative team has come up with stuff I never would have.

As I stated in an earlier chapter, summer is a great time to do a relationship series. A couple of summers ago, when I decided to do

---

36. Young, Ed, The Creative Leader: Unleashing the Power of Your Creative Potential, (Nashville, Tennessee: B&H Publishing Group, 2006), 173-174.

the "I Can't Get No Satisfaction" series, I challenged the creative team to give me some ideas on how to get the most out of it—everything from how to advertise it to how to teach it. Someone suggested that we get movie tickets printed with the name of the series and the title of the different messages on them and give them to our members to pass out across the city. Our graphic designer did such a good job with the tickets that people actually thought they were coming to a real movie. The tickets were made just like the ones at theaters and they read "Admit One." We had thousands of them printed and they were passed out all over the city.

That idea by my team got my creative juices flowing and I suggested that we continue the movie theme by putting real popcorn machines on the stage, the same kind you see behind the counter at movie theaters everywhere. We rented several of them and had popcorn popping in the narthex as they came in, as well as on the stage during my message. The whole church smelled like popcorn and we gave every member a bag as they left. Our people loved it and to this day it was the most successful series with regard to creativity that we have ever done. Like Young, I have benefited tremendously from surrounding myself with creative people to help our ministry stay ahead of the curve.

CHAPTER TEN

/ EXPANSION /

Many pastors who experience terrific numerical growth make the mistake of staying put. Churches are one of the few organizations that do not seem to grasp the importance of maximizing their growth potential. McDonald's, Wal-Mart, and most successful businesses in America are constantly looking for ways to expand. I would argue that you cannot drive ten minutes in any neighborhood without seeing a McDonald's. They add locations in any area they think people will patronize.

One of the major keys to the continued growth of "THE WORD" CHURCH has been our ability to stay ahead of the curve as it relates to expanding. From adding services to adding locations, we have never been afraid to expand the vision in order to accommodate the growth.

SEATING AND ATTENDANCE

I always know exactly how many people are in service because of my seating strategy. I don't care how large or small you are, always make sure people sit right next to each other starting from the front to the back. Put ropes up and only allow people to sit in the next available row. Organizing your seating process in this way suggests that you are planning to grow. Parishioners should think that they need to get accustomed to sitting right next to their neighbor because soon, every seat will be filled. It also allows you to count who is there, which is highly critical. You should always have someone count your crowd. You need a barometer of your growth. How can you plan and strategize if you do not know your numbers?

I ask every pastor I train when I first meet them the same question, "How many people are you preaching to each week?" I ask this question to get a sense of what they need from me. Some guys have great momentum and just need me to help them handle the growth and take it to the next level. Others are struggling to get anybody to come and are hoping I can give them some pragmatic principles and strategies to help build some momentum.

Large or small, you should know your average attendance if you are serious about continued growth. One pastor said to me that he does not count his crowd, he just ministers. I told him what I tell all pastors: numbers matter. There's even a book in the Bible called Numbers. When you are looking to grow and expand, you have to take attendance seriously and become intentional in building your weekly attendance. Count every person.

Seating people together also helps the flow of the service. When people come in late, they do not interrupt the service by walking down to the front or trying to squeeze past people who are already comfortably seated. You sit in the next available seat as you come in and no one is disturbed.

MULTIPLE SERVICES

We started our church in a high school that sat about 800 people. In one year, we went from about 100 to over 700 in attendance. One

Sunday, a few leaders hurriedly came to the area where I prepped for service to tell me that we had no more space to seat anyone. The floor and the balcony were full. People were even sitting on the stage, and would have to remain there while I preached. We decided to start a second service.

As I look back now, we actually waited too long to do it. You do not have to be full to start another service. If you are close to capacity and have momentum, go for it. Starting another service creates room for growth without having to spend any significant money. Starting another service also gives people options, which they love.

HOW EXACTLY DO YOU DO IT?

1. Gather your paid and unpaid staff and give them your vision for an additional service. Without their support, the task is close to impossible. A second service will require that they come earlier and in many cases stay later. Everyone will have to work a double shift. The goal is to have a different crew for each service, but the reality is, in the beginning, your key leaders will likely have to stay for both.

2. Make sure you choose a starting time that makes sense for your ministry. Traditionally, most churches launch their second service early, around 8:00 a.m. That is fine if you are attracting older, affluent individuals with no small children. If you are attracting people with small children, you might want to consider starting a later service, say around noon on Sundays. This gives the young crowd time to sleep in and get themselves and their kids ready without feeling rushed. My last weekend service starts at 1:00 p.m. and people are still late. Do not make the mistake of starting too early; know your demographic and who you appeal to.

3. Use the principles in the chapter on marketing to get the word out about your new service. Use slogans like, "Here we **grow** again!"

People love winners. When your people sense that you are winning and growing, they will begin telling everyone about the church they are so excited to be a part of. Start about six weeks out marketing your new service. People cannot come if they do not know.

4. Launch your second service on a major day like Easter, Mother's Day, New Year's Day, etc. These are days that attract bigger-than-usual crowds. Use that momentum for your new service.

5. Give something away for free. As you market your new service, announce that you will have bags of groceries, gas cards, shoes for children in need, or anything your ministry can afford. People like free stuff! Remember, they may come for the stuff, but God has a word for them when they get there and many of them will stay. It also shows them your commitment to outreach, which is what people want to see from the 21st century church.

6. Preach the same thing. Because you have two services does not mean you preach two different messages. Many pastors feel weird saying the same thing twice, or in my case, five times each weekend, but remember: though you may have multiple services, it is still one church that needs to hear the same word from God.

I preach the same sermon all weekend. I might add or subtract something according to the demographics and flow of each service, but the opening scripture, the subject, and the big points are always the same.

Have you ever gone to a great movie or play that you liked so much you wanted to see it again with a friend? What if the movie or the play was different when you went back? You would be disappointed because you were expecting the same movie. I have found over the years that my staff, leadership, and all those that sit through multiple services look forward to hearing it again. Preach the same thing.

Over the years, we have constantly added services, changed service times, and added or switched locations to accommodate our growing crowd. That is how you keep expanding. While we were in the high school, our times were 9:00 a.m. and 11:30 a.m. We then remodeled an old movie theater with a thousand-person seating capacity. We continued to grow so we changed our times to 7:30 a.m., 9:30 a.m., and 11:30 a.m. In less than six months time, we had to move to four services. The service times then were 7:00 a.m., 8:30 a.m., 10:00 a.m., and 11:30 a.m.

Because the theater we were worshiping in was connected to a small strip mall, the store owners complained that we were using up all the parking spaces and their customers could not park. It got so crowded that people were starting to park illegally, which caused many of them to get ticketed and some were even getting towed. When that started happening consistently, I knew we had to make another move or we would stunt our growth potential.

When you are growing, do whatever you have to do to make room for that growth, whether it is multiple services, renting or purchasing a larger facility, or using multiple locations. Do not kill your momentum because of a failure to expand.

Eventually, we purchased our current facility, which was the largest indoor sports arena in our area. Right away, we doubled in seating capacity and parking. Since being in our present facility, we have continued to grow to the point of needing four weekend services, including one on Saturday.

SATURDAY NIGHT LIVE

I have always enjoyed and appreciated the challenge of coming up with different ways to accommodate the crowds we have been blessed with. About three years ago, we decided to try a Saturday service. I must admit, I had a lot of trepidation about starting it. In all honesty, I have been a bit nervous every time we launched a new service.

To pastors contemplating adding a service or location, feelings of uncertainty are perfectly natural. I have always told my team that if it does not make you a little nervous, it is not a major move. I wondered if people would come to church in Cleveland on a Saturday, especially in the frigid winter months. The very first Saturday night service we held, we were full to capacity. Gradually, less people came and we have leveled out at about 500 people a week.

When we started our Saturday service, our target was the young, Hip-Hop crowd looking for something to do on Saturday night. However, we quickly discovered that we were drawing our most diverse crowd of the weekend on Saturday nights. We have more whites at our Saturday service than all of our Sunday services combined. For whatever reason, whites love it. Our Saturday crowd also attracts some of the best givers in our ministry. Whereas I thought it would attract the young, urban crowd, I have come to discover that the Saturday crowd is a lot like the 8:00 a.m. crowd. They are disciplined, business executives who love the idea of coming on Saturday night and having their Sundays to themselves.

Should you decide to start a Saturday service, it is a good idea to start no later than 6:00 p.m. and make the service no longer than an hour and 15 minutes. Parishioners look forward to getting out in about an hour and still having time to go to dinner or catch a movie.

MULTIPLE LOCATIONS

About three years ago, I sensed that we were not maximizing our growth potential. I was holding three services on Sunday, and one on Saturday night, and people were still joining by the tens each weekend. We come on local television Monday through Friday at 7:30 a.m. here in the Greater Cleveland area. Thousands of people wake up to our broadcast and consider me their television pastor in this area.

One day, it dawned on me that unlike McDonald's and Wal-Mart, we were not taking full advantage of our popularity and customer base. As I stated earlier, these powerhouse companies open locations everywhere possible. Why couldn't I do the same? If people knew that our church was within walking distance or a short drive from where they lived, why wouldn't they come?

I decided that we would open churches on all four sides of the city and that I would borrow the slogan of my good friend Bishop I.V. Hilliard who pastors New Light Church, a megachurch in Houston, Texas. Like me, he feels a call to his city and has churches all over Houston. Their slogan is, "We're not far from where you are!" As I mentioned in my chapter on facilities, we have come full circle by returning to the high school model of worship with our satellite locations.

What we discovered right away was that there were thousands of people who loved our church and wanted to come but they simply did not have the means to get there. Once they found out we had a satellite campus in their neighborhood, they came in droves.

A few years ago, our ministry felt some of the effects of the recession. People were losing jobs and some of our members were leaving Cleveland in search of better income for them and their families. At the end of one of the hardest financial years in recent American history, my CFO gave me our year-end report. To my amazement, we had raised as much money as we had the year before. Though our main location had taken a hit, we had made up the loss with the addition of our satellites. The new locations helped maintain our budget at a critical juncture.

Expanding to multiple locations not only adds new crowds, it also adds new offerings. As I stated previously, the more souls you get, the more offerings you get. The more offerings you get, the more it allows you to go after more lost souls.

When and if you do decide to open another location, make sure you do not use opening day as a barometer of the actual attendance. For us, the first weekend we start any new location is always standing room only because of nosy people, spies from other churches, etc. It takes about four to six weeks to see what you really have or to sort of level out. After that, you can then begin to estimate your realistic attendance and growth.

Do not lock yourself into anything in terms of longevity when you first start a new location. Call it a pilot service and inform your members that you are merely testing the waters. Let them know that you are going to try something for a few weeks or months, and trust God for the results. That way, if it turns out not to be a good move, you don't look as if you are indecisive or dithering in your decisions.

HOW CAN YOU BE AT ALL THESE LOCATIONS AT THE SAME TIME?

The question I am asked more than any other, is how I preach at all of our locations on the weekend. I will try to explain what we do as simply as possible. Our service times at our main location are Saturday at 6:00 p.m. and Sundays at 8:00 a.m., 10:00 a.m., and 1:00 p.m. We have satellite locations across the city in different high schools that all start at 11:45 am. Each week, while I am preaching the 10:00 a.m. service at the main location, I look into the camera and preach to the satellites at the same time. I even say things throughout the message to keep them engaged like, "To those watching us from our satellite locations…"

I am normally done with the 10:00 a.m. service no later than 11:30 a.m. Keep in mind, all the satellites start at 11:45 a.m. Once I am done preaching, a rep from my media department takes the mini DV from the 10:00 a.m. service and drives copies to all of our satellites so that the parishioners can watch me on screens we purchased for each location. While they are driving the message to the satellites, so that I can get through traffic quickly, a police sheriff drives me to one of the other satellites so I can preach in person.

Fifteen minutes is not a lot of time to travel the distance that I have to travel. What gives us the extra time we need to get the message and me to the locations is praise and worship, which lasts until we get there. Nearly a thousand people attend our satellite locations and they are fully aware that half the time I will not be there in person. They don't care if I am there or not because I have trained them to come for the Word and not me.

Do not underestimate the power of technology in the 21st century church. People today do not mind watching you onscreen. Their iPhones and iPads have screens, their laptop has a screen, the check-in kiosk at the airport has a screen, they watch television via screen, and they go to the movies and watch a screen. We have found that churchgoers are not bothered by watching me preach on a screen.

We have also discovered that though they do not mind watching the message onscreen, they appreciate live music and a live band which we deliver at all of our satellites. Though I am not there live, everyone else is. I am aware that many of you might choose to have just one satellite location you can preach at live. To those of you contemplating preaching by way of DVD, below are a few tips to help you.

- Purchase the proper media equipment. They must hear and see you clearly for this to work.

- Train a satellite liaison to touch and love the people when you cannot be there. This person is also in charge of making sure every facet of ministry runs smoothly, from parking to the reception of new members. They should make sure the satellite reflects you and the main location.

- Make sure your music is excellent. If you are not there live all the time, your music has to be tight to keep their mind off that reality. In most cases, you do not need a choir, just a good praise team and a strong professional band.

- If you are using the school model like us, open an office in the area where the school is located. It is important that people know you are not just there for offerings but to impact that particular community as well. Your liaison should report to and manage that office full-time if possible.

- The day you open and at least once a month, give away something for free. Groceries, gas cards, gift cards, etc. Call it In-Reach Weekend and watch the results. It costs you something, but it is the reason you are there. Do not ever forget that!

Also, my wife, Lady Vernon goes to one of the other satellites, and once I am done preaching via the screens, she comes up and gets the offering, makes big announcements, and hugs and touches the crowd for me. We go different directions during the satellite hour in order to touch all locations.

PLANTING PASTORS

I recently planted my first son in Akron, Ohio. After doing some research we noticed that we had over a thousand people coming from that area which is about 30 minutes away from Cleveland. I decided to keep expanding our brand by opening "WORD" Akron. I have a son in ministry that is simply a preaching machine. He has my heart and spirit, which is a necessary prerequisite.

After much prayer and training, I sent him to Akron as my campus pastor, not my liaison. The reason I gave him the title of pastor is because unlike the liaisons, he preaches each week and he is in another city. He needs the spiritual authority to take that area for God.

Though he preaches and teaches each weekend and Wednesday, he does not preach what he likes. He preaches my sermon from the week before. I e-mail him my notes each week, and he watches me preach the message on DVD so he can do it the same way. He is fully aware that though I trust him and have given him the opportunity of a lifetime, God gave me "THE WORD" CHURCH to watch over and I guard and protect our brand. Before he went, I made it crystal clear to both him and his beautiful wife that no matter how well things panned out (and they have), he was to never forget that he is not the senior pastor and it is not his ministry.

The first weekend we opened the Akron location over 2,000 people showed up. Our television program comes on in that city so they were quite familiar with our brand. As per usual, on opening day we gave away trucks full of groceries and school supplies for children in need. Because of all of my obligations to my locations in Cleveland I am barely ever there, but my son is doing a fantastic job. His leadership and our commitment to expansion and evangelism combined have led to having to add a second service.

All the offerings from the Akron location come back to the main house. Also, my wife and I go to Akron whenever there is a fifth weekend for something we call "Senior Pastor Sunday," where I preach to both services at the Akron church in order to maintain the connection with them. I do this as a precautionary measure in the event we have to remove the campus pastor for any reason, whether it is disloyalty, immorality, or just life period. It is important that my wife and I stay connected to all our locations so that we are not strangers in our own church. Even though he preaches on a regular basis, one Wednesday and one weekend a month, as opposed to him preaching live, they watch me on the screens. Again, this is not any knock against the campus pastor; I would not have sent him If I did not trust him, but it is important that I always stay connected.

As I am writing this, we have plans to open our next location this year in another area of Northeastern Ohio, and I have no plans to stop expanding anytime soon. My vision is for "THE WORD" CHURCH to be within 15 minutes from wherever you live in the Greater Cleveland area. Any pastor with good momentum should consider expanding however the Lord leads.

I recently preached to my Akron church for the first time in about four months. About 70 people walked down the aisle for salvation or rededication, and the offering was nearly double what it normally is. That night I was humbled, and my wife and I were reminded of the power of the senior pastor. No matter how gifted your associates are, they are not you. Every church you have, you must stay connected for its maximum success.

Keep in mind the model that I am promoting. Some of you might release a pastor and give him total autonomy over the location. Right now, I'm not there. I feel led to lead a spiritual dynasty. Ultimately, we'll have dozens of churches connected to the main church. We feel "THE WORD" CHURCH name and brand has power and that in this area, my name and brand has power.

My goal is to go to each church at least once every four to six weeks. Though my son is doing a wonderful job, I stay connected. If I have learned anything over the years, no matter how great your staff person or employee might be, no one loves it like you. It was birthed out of you. "THE WORD" CHURCH is not only my spiritual assignment; it's how I feed my family. I don't allow anyone to water it down. No one does what you expect, they do what you inspect. This is no knock against the sons and daughters who I plant. I inform them that they can start their own church whenever they want, but this is the dream my wife and I chose to pursue, and they are a part of it.

WHAT IS YOUR MODEL?

One model for ministry expansion is complete autonomy. In this model, the mother church invests in a baby church. They continue the spirit and legacy of the host church, but they do things their way and return a percentage of their offerings to the mother church. The other model is the one that we embrace, the replication model. The satellites are replicas and extensions of the main church and therefore mimic everything the main church does. There are benefits to both models, but I can better explain the advantages of the latter model since that's the one we utilize.

Satellite pastors don't have to prepare messages. I do the research, I preach it, and they stay a week behind me. The time they don't have to spend doing research and deep exegesis, they can touch the community.

My son in Akron lives in a comfortable home in a nice suburb. When we planted him, we gave him a new vehicle at no cost, and we cover the maintenance. It is important to me that the pastors I plant worry about their location and not their bills. They have financial security and they get a chance to pastor without having the pressure that I have. They still have the full support and access to the resources of the main house. You must determine which model you will use. There might come a time or a season where I transition to the other model, but at this time, that season has not yet come.

SIZE DOES MATTER

CHAPTER ELEVEN

/ IT'S THE WEEKEND, STUPID /

A few years ago, I borrowed the following phrase from a chapter in Ed Young's book, *The Creative Leader*: "It's the weekend, Stupid." Incidentally, he admits to gleaning the phrase from James Carville, a member of former President Bill Clinton's administration, who hung a sign in front of his desk that said, "It's the economy, Stupid." The realization Young came to that I have come to in my own life, is that you must recognize what's important and focus on perfecting that. For pastors, it's the weekend, the one or two days a week when we have service and see the majority of our congregation. That's what it all comes down to; that's why we do everything that we do. Everything is centered on the weekend services.

My team and I spend hours preparing for our weekend services. Each one is something like, if not actually, a production. The video, music, arts—every aspect—have to be deliberately planned out. Sound levels must be precise (no hissing in the mic) and the camera angles have to be accurate. My minister of music knows what I'm preaching, and when appropriate, tailors the songs the praise team and choir sing to my message. He sends out a detailed layout of the order of service for the weekend to every staff member who needs it. The creative arts ministry is informed of my sermon series and develops dramatic presentations based on my teachings. My campus liaisons and key members of my staff get electronic copies of my sermon notes in advance so that in the event some unfortunate incident occurs, there are others prepared to preach the same thing I would have. It also gives our children's and teen ministry leaders the tools they need to stay in line with me, so that families are all being taught the same thing.

We have a children's church so that parents can receive the Word of God and not be concerned with their children's needs while they're in service, and also so that children can be taught in a manner appropriate for their age. To ensure the kids' safety, we conduct background checks on everyone who volunteers in our children's ministry.

I know that every parent is concerned about where their kids are going for an hour, especially for first-time visitors who are unfamiliar with our church. So, for those who don't feel comfortable parting with their children for a short time, we have a baby section in a rear corner of the church. People with small children are not allowed to sit in the front of our church because it can be distracting to others, and cause them to miss out on crucial information. Our ushers will ask parents of children who are crying to step out for a moment. In addition to the fact that screaming babies can be disturbing to others nearby, we record our services for national television. I doubt if our viewing audience tune in to hear the babies in my church cry.

MUSIC MINISTRY

There are many places that pastors cut corners on, and I understand. When you're growing and growing fast, sometimes you have to. But don't cut corners in your music department. People listen to quality music all the time on their local radio station, via satellite, on their iPods, etc., but, more importantly, music adds another dimension to your worship experience. The two work in concert with each other.

You need the best musicians you can afford and a skilled minister of music who is spiritual and involved. Every musician won't have the spiritual depth you might want, but your minister of music should. She'll be the one leading your congregation into worship and can help or hinder the flow of the service. Make sure she attends staff meetings and connects with the other staff members as necessary to ensure that she's in tune with the team.

Sometimes, the music department is viewed as self-regulating and separate from the other areas of ministry, but that kind of thinking is antiquated and flawed. You need all your department managers functioning cohesively and they won't if they are not held to the same accountability standards.

The music ministry is vital to your weekend services. Don't go the cheap route. Spend some money and hire accomplished musicians.

THE DEVIL IS IN THE DETAILS

Ask anyone on my staff if I'm very detailed when it comes to ministry and they will probably answer you by telling you that "very detailed" is somewhat of an understatement. A better designation is probably that I'm overly detailed, and I don't apologize for that. When it comes to God's people and the ministry He's given me, I want things to be first-rate, and I will go to great lengths to ensure that it is.

I talked about staffing in an earlier chapter, and I mentioned that I hire competent people, people who are smarter than me in their particular area of expertise. I have to have people who know what they're doing because things must be excellent. Business owners and corporate executives attend my services. Therefore, they expect a certain level of professionalism when they attend. People should not feel like they are stepping down a notch when they visit your church.

On the contrary, they should expect a level of service and professionalism equal to or better than what they experience in their daily lives going to work, conducting personal business, etc. Remember, it doesn't matter what else is good if your weekend services are not, and they won't be if you don't pay attention to the details.

Most ministries who have grown to this level have done so because they are concerned with the details. Many smaller churches who just want to be "led by the spirit" impede their growth by ignoring the small factors that affect their church's development.

Pay attention to everything. Your church's marketing materials, website, and printed documents should be free of errors, user-friendly, and visually appealing. The hallways should smell fresh and the bathrooms should be immaculate. Regardless of the season, the thermostat should reflect a moderate, comfortable temperature. The information center should be stocked, but not overstocked, with important information about your church, and where to get more information about unadvertised programs, services, and resources. For example, always have a general flyer available pushing people to peruse your website to find out about upcoming events and ways to get involved in ministry.

I know it can be irritating at times, but any staff person will tell you that we are better because of my focus on detail. I realize that no matter how hard I try, things are never going to be completely perfect, but my overall goal is to create and maintain a spirit of excellence.

THE CHIEF MINISTRY OFFICER

Because our volunteer staff is so integral to the success of our services, I had to designate a person to provide oversight, direction, and leadership for our ministry department. This person is called our

CMO, or Chief Ministry Officer. A growing ministry requires someone full-time who is not thinking about anything except ministry.

All the leaders of the individual ministries report to our CMO and she reports back to me. If something goes wrong during our services, I go to the CMO, not the individual leader. I don't have time to chase the issue down that far. I expect my CMO to have the pulse of the ministries and be able to give an account of them when I ask.

LET MINISTRY DICTATE STRUCTURE

One of the mistakes I made when I was in my earlier years of ministry was trying to come up with a whole lot of stuff for people to do. I had ministries for drug dealers and ministries for college students; ministries for women with kids and ministries for women without kids; ministries for men with video game addictions and ministries for men with Napoleon complexes—okay, maybe I'm exaggerating a bit. But at one point, I did start a ministry for young guys from urban areas because a lot of them were frequenting our ministry. The ministry was called the "T.H.U.G." Ministry (Transformed Hearts Under God). While the ministry went strong for awhile, eventually, as attendance began to taper, I realized the need for this particular ministry had waned.

I started a couple dozen ministries because they sounded like good ideas, and I wanted to meet the needs of as many people as possible. I began to stress over suitable ministry leaders, classroom space, and scheduling. It's funny when I think about it now, but I remember meetings where my staff would debate about which ministry should displace another for meeting space, when there were only five people showing up for each of them. While nobody was showing up for the Foreign Language ministry meetings, 300 people were at the Outreach ministry meeting.

And then it hit me. Ministry should necessitate, and resultantly dictate, structure. I was stressing about coming up with space that I didn't even need. Why should I try to find or build space for groups that weren't supported by even one percent of our population? On the other hand, if I have several hundred people showing up for a ministry meeting, I need to have space to accommodate them.

When I first opened our Akron location, my son who I planted there asked me, "Pastor, what are the goals?" I said, "Only to save souls and do outreach." He was somewhat puzzled. "What about ministries?" he inquired. "No ministries," I replied. "Let's get there and see what we have, see what the needs are. We'll wrap structure around that."

When they first start, many pastors sit down with their wives or with their leaders and try to create 15 different ministries to offer before they even know who's coming to their church. That's just not smart. Wait until you see who is coming to your church, get a sense of what ministries would be helpful to them, and then formulate a structure. Don't stress about trying to come up with ministry options until you know what people need or would like to have.

It took me three years after the opening of two of our satellite locations before I settled on opening offices in the neighborhoods where they are. I didn't immediately open administrative offices because I didn't know if people would even show up to church. I wanted to observe and get an impression of whether the satellite locations warranted administrative facilities. Only after I had properly assessed the situations and determined there was a need did we open offices.

I'm not saying don't try new things. You should always challenge yourself and your team to come up with more ways of encouraging participation from your members. Ministry involvement is key for any growing church. People give more of their time and money when they feel connected to a particular cause.

What I am saying is don't come up with an idea for ministry and then spend an unreasonable amount of your human and financial resources to implement it before you know there is a real market for it. Let your ministry needs determine your ministry structure.

THE WELCOME TEAM AND FIRST TOUCH MINISTRIES

After several discussions with my team regarding ways to improve our level of service to attendees, we came up with a new way of referring to the volunteers who serve in highly visible positions, and who have to interact with every person who enters our building and parking lot. These individuals mainly include ushers, greeters, and parking attendants, but include a few other volunteer groups as well. When our ministry first started, we looked at each of these ministries discretely, and each of them had a separate function. That's no longer the case. We now look at them as one unit, and collectively we call them "The Welcome Team." The ministries that make up The Welcome Team are called "First Touch" ministries.

You have one chance to make a first impression. First Touch volunteers are the first people visitors see when they come to your church, and every person who takes a seat in your sanctuary comes in contact with them before they sit. They must be effervescent. They need to look pleasant, smell pleasant, and have nice breath. Women need to go out of their way to dress modestly; men don't need to see a woman who looks overtly sexual when they come to church. We inspect the clothing of our women. If something is too tight or too revealing, we ask them not to serve that day. First Touch volunteers need to smile, hug, and have loving attitudes.

People who serve in these positions can make or break your church. They set the tone for a visitor's experience. If the parking lot attendant yells at them to move along quickly, a greeter looks at them condescendingly, or an usher angrily instructs them to get to their seat, they will find another place to worship. Have you ever thought about how many people may have decided not to join your church because of the disposition of the driver who transported them from a remote parking lot? Or how many visitors may have discouraged other potential visitors from coming because they told them how mean the ushers were at your church?

Cautiously select individuals to serve on First Touch ministries. Their role is an important one. Just as they can stunt your growth by being disagreeable, they can increase your growth by being amiable. A person may never make it up to the front of the church to speak to you, but if they are showered with love from the beginning of their visit, they'll likely base their opinion of your ministry on the kindness they were shown by your First Touch volunteers.

First Touch ministries obviously aren't for everybody, but that does not mean a person can't be involved. They simply need to find another ministry with different requirements or that is more suitable for their personality or skill set.

The Welcome Team volunteers who work inside wear bright red badges with bold, scripted white letters that read "Welcome!" They are required to wear the badges anytime and anywhere they serve. They also wear coordinating colors to symbolize their unity.

Having the First Touch ministries work together as one team also has another benefit. We've cross-trained them so that if we're short on ushers for one service, we can grab a greeter and have them usher instead, and vice versa. Requiring the ministry volunteers to be versed in several different positions was an important change for our organization. Before, when we were alerted that someone was unable to serve an hour or less before service, we'd have to scramble to find replacement volunteers to come in and serve during a shift they weren't scheduled for. Now? We simply pull someone from another ministry already at service who has been cross-trained. But wouldn't that leave the other ministry shorthanded? No. We almost always have extra volunteers on hand that we can grab from somewhere to serve, and that is precisely the point of cross- training. What good is it to have a surplus of volunteers if they are unfamiliar with how to serve in other capacities where needed? I think you get the point, but if you don't, cross-train your volunteers.

Most of our staff have Mondays and Fridays off and work Saturdays and Sundays instead. By now you know why. It's the weekend that matters. These are the most crucial days of the week for us, far more important than Monday and Friday because it's when our members show up—and give money. If people don't give offerings, you don't have a church.

With the exception of an emergency, my staff is not allowed to take personal days on the weekends. I constantly reiterate to them that our members pay our salaries and they are most important. While our people don't officially vote, I tell our staff that they do unofficially cast their ballots—with their presence and with their giving. They will vote favorably or unfavorably, and the difference between the two will be clear based on the rise or fall of your attendance and offerings.

The magnitude of what you do on the weekends, your volunteer power, the connectivity and synergy of your staff, the timeliness of your messages, and the creativity of your worship experience contribute to the type of environment your attendees will enjoy or endure. Put some serious time and thought into planning and preparing for your weekend services.

An hour before church, our staff is required to greet, hug, and smile at the members when they come in through the main doors. We form a line on both sides of our lobby area, and we call it "The

Tunnel of Love." Showering our members with affection makes them feel at home and lets them know how happy we are to see them. It also encourages and sets the tone for an atmosphere of love that permeates the entire organization.

And let's not forget about Wednesday, which is also a highly important service day. At "THE WORD" CHURCH, our pecking order goes something like this: weekend, Wednesday, weekday. In other words, in terms of priority, our primary focus is the weekend, then Wednesday, and then the other weekdays. And we don't ever cancel service. Nope, not even in bad weather. There are still dedicated, faithful members who want the Word, and want to come to their church when the weather is bad. We're a hospital for the spiritually sick, and hospitals don't close because there's a snowstorm.

For those who just cannot get out of their driveway, we do offer the option of watching service on the Internet. We only stream in times of inclement weather. I know there are many megachurch ministries who stream all of their services, but at this time, I don't feel led to do that. For national and international ministries, that makes sense. We're the city's church, and I want them in one of our buildings on the weekends, not in the bed with their laptop.

ASK ME ANYTHING

A couple of years ago, I came up with a concept for our information area that highlighted its main purpose, which was to be the place that people can come to find out anything they want about our ministry. I called this concept "Ask Me Anything," and aptly applied the title to our resource centers at every location. I also had our graphic designer create an "Ask Me Anything" badge consistent with the signage we use for our information areas that all of our key staff members are required to wear anytime we have service. This has proven to work really well. The badges are larger than normal and easily visible from a distance, making it easier for our attendees to identify who they can go to when they have a question or concern.

The staff who wear the badges are well-versed in everything that we have going on at any given time, but in the event they can't answer a question, they know it's never acceptable to say "I don't know," unless it's followed by, "but I'll find out who does" or "I'll get the answer for you." There are certain staff members who are not required to wear a badge because during service times, their focus has to be on a specific area of ministry, and I don't want them distracted or pulled away from their duties because a member needs to know where they can find a water fountain. For example, our ministry's security detail is responsible for making sure the members are kept safe during our services, which means they have to constantly scan the audience and be aware of any suspicious activity. If they're inundated with questions from members, it takes their focus away from member safety and leaves the ministry vulnerable to a person with impure motives desiring to cause harm. Therefore, we give Ask Me Anything badges to only those who are knowledgeable about our ministry and who can provide advice without compromising the excellence of another area of ministry.

Many churches call the information area "the information area" or "guest services" or something like that. But Ask Me Anything is a catchy name that implies your ability to address any question a person may have, and is more visitor-friendly. Consider borrowing this concept or coming up with one of your own so that members and visitors can easily identify who can answer their questions or where they can go for information.

THE DISNEYWORLD EXPERIENCE

Even if you've never been to Disneyworld, you know that it is one of the most familiar places in the world. Disney is a brand that has had remarkable success. Like many people, my first perception of Disneyworld was based on what I had heard and seen on television. When I actually had the opportunity to visit however, my perception changed dramatically.

The parking lot was full, causing us to have to park near the back and walk. The lines to get on rides or see feature attractions were hours long and it was extremely crowded. These are major inconveniences even for the most easygoing person. Yet, no one seemed to mind. I quickly found out why most people weren't annoyed by things that would normally be nuisances. They didn't really notice.

Disney has done a masterful job of creating an experience. They make sure that from the time you get out of your car till you're ready to leave the park, your focus is directed toward pleasantries that distract you from your inconveniences. The shuttles have welcoming themes and friendly drivers. The employees are courteous and service is efficient. While you wait in line, there are mini-shows going on around you, or entertaining television programs viewable from your position to give you something to watch. They employ all sorts of creativity to promote an atmosphere of fun, happiness, and excitement. And it works. People bring their families year after year and spend hundreds (sometimes thousands) of dollars to stand in two-hour lines for a ride that lasts two minutes or less. By the end of the day, they've only had an opportunity to enjoy five or six rides and maybe a show or two, but they keep coming back because they enjoy the experience.

There is a lot we can learn from Walt Disney. Craft an experience for your attendees by coming up with creative ways to engage them from the moment they arrive at your ministry. If you use shuttles to transport your members from remote parking lots, play pleasant music while they ride, or even better, record a CD with information about what people can expect when they actually get inside, or little known facts about your ministry. Have a looping video showing on TVs throughout your narthex or lobby area with announcements relevant to your members so you don't have to spend too much time doing it in service.

There is a parallel to be drawn between Disney and the mega-church. There are inconveniences that people might have to tolerate when they visit mega ministries. Getting out of the parking lot in a timely manner, possibly having to sit in the overflow area if services are particularly packed, and having to wait in long lines to speak with the pastor after church, are all probable drawbacks of visiting a megachurch. However, these drawbacks will pale in comparison to the benefits parishioners receive when they attend, if you make a conscientious effort to reduce inconveniences by designing a rewarding experience. After all, they get a few rides and a few laughs at Disneyworld. You're promoting the best product ever—Jesus Christ. Ask a member of "THE WORD" CHURCH what inconveniences they have when they attend, and you'll probably get a lot of confused looks. Why? Because they don't see any of the things I mentioned as inconveniences. They don't notice. The worship is spirited, the Word is sound, and the workers are sincere. That's what they care about at the end of the day and for that reason, that's what you should care about.

Just like a family vacation at Disneyworld, Wednesdays and weekends are special occasions. Your members and visitors are the VIP guests. They deserve the red carpet and the five-star service. Go above and beyond to treat your members as if they matter and they will come back week after week, and tell others about what a wonderful church they go to. They'll encourage other people to come, informing them that there is no church like yours. Soon your services will be thriving and overflowing, and people will feel like they can't afford to miss. This will translate to consistently increasing attendance and offerings, and thus increased ability to do more for God's Kingdom. As long as you keep creating experiences, the cycle will continue to expand and you'll be in a powerful position to take your city (and beyond) for Christ.

SIZE DOES MATTER

CHAPTER TWELVE

/ EDUCATION /

I am not sure where, but I remember reading a quote from Dr. King regarding education: "The function of education is to teach one to think intensively and to think critically... Intelligence plus character—that is the goal of true education."

Over the last six years, I have become an apologist for the necessity of pastors pursuing a seminary education if possible. By no means am I suggesting that you cannot do effective and impactful ministry without it. History has proven that to be an untruth. However, very few pastors go to seminary after reaching the megachurch status. As much as I have traveled and interacted with megachurch leaders, I have never met one like me, who decided to go to seminary after reaching this level of church growth. Having now matriculated through seminary, I can say not only theoretically but experientially that education has improved both me and the congregation I pastor immensely.

MY JOURNEY

About six years ago, I was on the phone with Dr. C. Jay Matthews, a good friend and a prominent pastor in our city. He said to me, "Vernon,

God has blessed you with the largest black church in our city and given you influence that cannot be denied. There is only one thing you are missing, my friend. You should consider a seminary education." I had been in and out of school for over a decade, but I never had the discipline to complete it. That phone conversation led to him introducing me to a man and a place that would enhance my destiny and the destiny of those around me for years to come. The man (who I mentioned earlier) was Dr. William H. Myers, Professor of New Testament and Black Church Studies at Ashland Theological Seminary, and the place was the McCreary Center for African American Religious Studies here in Cleveland, where he is President, Founder, Chairman, and CEO.

Dr. Myers created a diploma program sanctioned and accepted by Ashland for pastors like me. At the time, I did not have a bachelor's degree but I wanted to go to seminary. The diploma program normally takes two years, but I doubled my class load and finished in one. Without a break, I went straight through to the master's program at Ashland and aggressively completed it in two years. I am one of only three individuals that went from the diploma program to the completion of a Doctorate of Ministry degree.

MY PREACHING

Without question, education has improved my preaching. It has more depth, and it is much more substantive and prophetic in its presentation. I have so much more to draw from because of my training. I have read more scholarly books over the last five years than I have in the thirty-five previous years of my life. I now listen to sermons I preached before I went to school and cringe. It is amazing the liberties you take with a text when you have not been trained.

Let me make myself clear here. I had over 5,000 people in our church database before I ever went to seminary. God can and is using hundreds of pastors who are not formally educated. Who could deny the impact of Bishop T.D. Jakes who God is using to counsel presidents and lead a church of over 20,000 in Dallas, Texas, along with the many philanthropic endeavors he has taken on across the world? At the same time, every pastor should want to be his or her best for their congregation.

Education can only improve you as a pastor. I want to debunk all the myths that suggest that formal education takes away your power—that somehow you become rigid and lose your edge. Formal training has only made me better. It has allowed me to preach relevantly to the broken and to the triumphant. I can now preach in prisons to convicted felons or lecture at a university to a room full of professors.

THE IMPACT OF EDUCATION

Since I decided to pursue education, the impact on my ministry has been incredible. Hundreds of my members, pastors that I mentor, and even family members have gone back to school. At least one person each weekend at one of our locations brings me a copy of a degree or certificate from some institution of higher learning. I had no idea that my pursuing education would impact so many people I touch. I would say to every person reading this, especially pastors or those leaning toward spiritual leadership, go to school! Do not let anyone minimize the effect education has on both you and those who follow and look up to you.

MAKE IT MANDATORY

When I sensed God's call on my life to preach, I did what people traditionally do in the Baptist denomination I was reared in. I went to my pastor with the expectation of him giving me a date to preach my initial or "trial" sermon. A few months after I told him I was called, I was up preaching my first public sermon, and the same night, after a majority vote of the church, I was a licensed minister. Three years later I was ordained. Not one time did my pastor or anyone else in our church even mention to me the need for formal training. My pastor had no formal training and neither did his pastor, so of course, he did not challenge me or hold me accountable in that area. The Baptist denomination, unlike our A.M.E. brothers and sisters, did not have any educational requirements for licensing and ordination. To their credit, the A.M.E. church has always placed high emphasis on academic excellence. In their book, *The Black Church in the African American Experience*, C. Eric Lincoln and Lawrence H. Mamiya write:

> From the beginning, the A.M.E. Church was concerned with providing social service relief to those in need. Today, the church maintains seven housing projects in as many cities across America to help house the needy in settings conducive to Christian social development. An equally strong interest of the emergent A.M.E. Church was education. The church leaders were not educated people, but they had a clear perception of what education would mean to the interest of the church and the advancement of the African people then held in abject slavery.[37]

Because I pursued and completed seminary, it allowed me the right to make education a prerequisite for all ministers in our ministry. I do not license anyone who does not have at least the minimum requirement of a Diploma of Theology offered at The McCreary Center in our city. No exceptions.

---

37. Lincoln, C. Eric, and Lawrence H. Mamiya, The Black Church in the African American Experience, (London: Duke University Press, 1990), 51.

TRAINED STAFF

Not only my ministers, but 95% of my staff is degreed. When you lead a megachurch or growing church you need skilled people. Earlier in my ministry, I minimized the importance of hiring degreed people. There are certain positions on your staff that require formal training—period. My CFO has a master's in business, my Executive Assistant has a master's in English, my youth minister has a bachelor's degree and is pursuing his master's, my head counselor has two master's degrees in counseling and is one year away from her Ph.D. All of my staff elders that assist with preaching and pastoral guidance have a Diploma of Theology.

To any pastor or person reading this who is interested in pursuing seminary training at an accredited and respected institution, I highly recommend you contact Dr. Myers at the McCreary Center in Cleveland. The website is www.mccrearycenter.org. If the McCreary Center is not your best option, he will direct you to a respected school in your area. Six years ago, I had nothing but a high school diploma; today I have a doctorate degree.

To those who say your schedule will not allow for school consider this: I am married with a young family including a newborn daughter. I pastor over 7,000 active members; more than double that number have joined our church. I preach eight or nine services a week in several different locations. I have a fellowship with over 100 senior pastors across the nation who I mentor and counsel.

The last year of my master's program, I was invited to about 30 cities to minster. It was the perfect storm. It was so crazy that I would preach Friday night in another city and have an all-day Saturday class that began at 8:00 a.m. Because we leased a small plane for our east coast trips, I would literally get through preaching in North Carolina at 9:00 p.m., hug people and sign my book until 10:00 p.m., jump on the plane and fly through the night.

SIZE DOES MATTER

On many Friday nights, we would land the plane at a little, country, one-lane airport in Ashland, Ohio. One of my staff members would meet us at the airport well after midnight and drive me over to the Holiday Inn Express in Ashland. I would lie down for a couple of hours and would be sitting in class by 8:00 a.m. I would remain in class until 4:00 p.m., then, my team would rush me back to Cleveland in 40 minutes because we have a weekly Saturday night service that begins at 6:00 p.m. I think you get the point. With all the aforementioned responsibilities and schedule conflicts, I never missed a quarter of school in six years and I never dropped or failed a class. You can do it!

CHAPTER THIRTEEN

/ PITFALLS TO AVOID /

In my attempt to help pastors everywhere reach their maximum growth potential, I have given you some of the major strategies and principles that I feel have contributed to us becoming and remaining a megachurch, in addition of course, to the providential hand of God. I sincerely believe that though God ultimately decides how many people join any church, in many cases, our lack of growth and momentum is caused by stagnant passivity and a deadening complacency. It is not God's fault if your church does not grow, nor is it His will. He expects you, as the leader, to do everything you can to make it happen and then trust Him for good results.

Most of what you have read in this book came as a direct result of prior failure. By no means do I have leading a megachurch figured out. Each day presents me with new challenges and new opportunities to fail at something. I truly believe it is my many failures and mistakes that made this book possible.

When my wife and I started "THE WORD" CHURCH in 2000, I was 30 years old, had just gotten married and had my first child, and my first church had just locked me out. I was young, confused, and without any denominational support because of my choice to be an independent ministry. A few nights after they had locked me out of my first church, I got a call from a pastor I had never met named Bishop Joey Johnson, who pastors The House of The Lord in Akron, Ohio. My wife, who knew I was lost and confused concerning what my next move in ministry should be after being locked out, had been sneaking to their women's Bible study and had asked his wife to have him give me a call.

After he introduced himself to me, I shared with him that it was only a few disgruntled deacons and trustees who had plotted my dismissal and that the majority of the church was still behind me. I also shared with him how the matter of me returning to that church as the pastor would ultimately be settled in court. I will never forget his response.

He asked me a question that changed my view of ministry forever. He said, "Let me ask you something. If you go to court and win, what have you really won? All you have won is the right to go back and fight." He explained to me how the stakeholders of that traditional church, with their history of turmoil, would do whatever it took to maintain power. He then gave me some powerful, life-changing advice. He said, "If I were you, I would start my own church." I followed that advice and the rest is history.

WHO ARE YOU UNDER?

Do not tell me how many people you are over until you tell me whom you are under. I am under Bishop Joey Johnson. God sent him into my life not just to give me a word about birthing my own ministry, but also to teach me patience, cover me, and keep me accountable. I could spend a whole chapter telling you how much I love him and what he means to me. My wife and I would probably be divorced without his guidance and without question, the stress and pressure that accompanies leading a megachurch would have been overwhelming without his guidance and support.

I believe a major mistake many pastors make is not praying for and seeking covering. Every pastor needs a pastor, someone to speak into your life and hold you accountable. Bishop Joey is crucial to my sanity and mental health both as a pastor and as a man trying to be the best husband and father I can be.

NO DEBT

If I could do it all over again, I would have never borrowed money for our building or anything else. I would have kept saving and bought everything with cash as we could afford it. It is so tempting to borrow money when you are experiencing exponential growth, but my advice to pastors is to keep your ministry free of debt. When you don't owe anyone anything, that's one less problem you have to deal with. When offerings inevitably fluctuate, you are not as worried as the pastor whose ministry is in debt.

Decide now that you and your church will not borrow money no matter how tempting it may be. Initially, this will require some major sacrifices by you and your congregation but the payoff will be worth it. Dave Ramsey says in *The Total Money Makeover*, "If you live like no one else, later you can live like no one else."[38]

Can you imagine your church raising millions of dollars with really no overhead other than utilities and salaries? Everything else can be poured into ministry. Do what you can to remain or become debt free.

FAIL-PROOF YOUR CHURCH

Did you ever consider the fact that you may not be pastoring forever? Or, God forbid, that you might have a moral failure? What

---

38. Ramsey, Dave, The Total Money Makeover, (Nashville: Thomas Nelson Inc., 2003), 1.

about if something happens and God calls you home a little earlier than you expect? I'm aware that this is somewhat taboo to talk about, but it is necessary nonetheless. What's the plan? Who is going to take over? What's the transition time? What if you mess up spiritually in a way that cannot be kept discreet?

Certainly as pastors and church leaders we're bound to have moral indiscretions that we too have to confess and repent for. We have to crucify our flesh daily just as we admonish our members to do. Most times, our sins are between God and us. But what happens when others are involved and privacy regarding the matter is not likely? Who leads while you await restoration? What if the magnitude of the mistake precludes restoration back to the original position? Then what?

These are tough questions, but ones you should already know the answer to if you are pastoring, or even considering pastoring. Things happen, and if you are serious about your call to ministry and the flock God has given you, you should have a contingency plan in place so that the work of the organization goes on even if you are not there for one reason or another.

You want your church to be purpose-driven (a great book and tenet promoted by Rick Warren), not personality-driven, so that it doesn't completely fall apart if you're not there. If you cannot answer the aforementioned questions, I suggest you shift priorities and move this one up a few notches. If you're unsure about how to go about it, seek the advice of your spiritual covering, and/or a legal professional who specializes in church contingency planning.

HIRE SLOWLY AND CAREFULLY

I am very patient and prayerful before hiring people on staff. In the past, I have hired much too quickly, and as a result we have had to part with several people. I have already discussed the three Cs of hiring in my chapter on staffing. No matter how fast you are growing, be prayerful about adding full-time staff, because when they don't work out and you have to let them go, it's very painful for both you and the person you are letting go. No matter how much they try, they cannot separate you as the CEO from you the pastor. The pastor loves you but the CEO has to fire you.

I have had to let people go who I loved to guard and protect our brand and ministry. Experience has also taught me to avoid hiring family and close friends. In many cases, it is hard for someone who knew you back when to see you as their boss today. I hired one of my best friends when we started "THE WORD." We were growing fast and all I wanted was someone I could trust on staff with me. As much as I loved him, he could not handle taking orders nor rebuke from me. He did not see me as his boss, he saw me as his friend.

After several warnings and doing all I could to save him, I made the painful but necessary decision to fire him. Since then, I have made several attempts to repair the relationship, but he still avoids me for the most part. In essence, by hiring him on staff, I lost him as a friend. I regret that.

Another issue with hiring too quickly is that you have to give them severance when they leave. Well, I suppose technically you don't have to but in my opinion, the integrity of your ministry dictates that you never drop anyone. If you made the mistake of hiring the wrong person, I believe you should write them a fair goodbye check. In most cases they have a family, house note, cost of living expenses, and so on. So that you can sleep at night, and to show that your ministry is one of class and grace, write the check. When you have written enough of those big goodbye checks, it causes you to be a lot more careful with whom you hire because of the painful and expensive process of letting them go.

I would also recommend that you never hire couples. It is extremely awkward and uncomfortable to be in a staff meeting and have to correct or discipline someone's spouse with them sitting there. Even worse is when you have to let one of them go. Can you ever trust a staff person after you have fired their spouse? In most cases, you end up having to fire both of them, which means you took all the income out of their home in one day. Though ultimately the firing is justified because of the employee's actions, no pastor wants that burden on them.

GET SCHOOL OUT OF THE WAY

The last six years have taken a great toll on me, both mentally and physically. Pursuing my diploma, master's, and doctorate degree while leading a megachurch with all its demands, has been arduous, to say the least. Knowing what I know now, I would have completed my education before we exploded. My advice to pastors is to realize the value of seminary education and get it out of the way as soon as possible.

Who knows what God has planned for your church? As the ministry grows, the demands on your time do too. Attending classes, reading scholarly books, writing papers, and leading a staff of 50 while preaching 8 or 9 services a week, is more than a notion. To young aspiring pastors and to pastors in general, go now and get it over with. Though a part of me regrets not having gone to school earlier, the fact that I am doing it now has inspired hundreds of our people to complete or begin their education, which makes the journey even more worthwhile.

IT WAS WORTH IT

I have a son in Birmingham, Alabama that I cover. A year ago, he was averaging 30 people in attendance, this past New Year's Eve, he had over 3,000 people in 2 services. He is growing like crazy, and I am so grateful that the mistakes we made have resulted in him and his ministry steering clear of the same pitfalls.

I pray that sharing the mistakes I have made will help you to avoid them. I do not have a lot of regrets; the failures and successes I've experienced are equally a part of the worthwhile journey of leading a megachurch.